Praise for Todd Davis

It's time to recognize what an important voice in American poetry we have in Todd Davis. —*Image*

Todd Davis is one of America's most capacious and imaginative poets. —Adrian Matejka, editor of *Poetry* and author of *Somebody Else Sold the World*

Reading Todd Davis's gorgeous poems, you can't help but feel that the capacities of human vision, and also our appetite for exactly this way of seeing and naming, have been mysteriously, precisely increased. —Jane Hirshfield, author of *The Asking* and *Ledger*

The poems . . . hold quiet wisdom, not unlike the solemnity and silence of personal prayer. —*Los Angeles Review of Books*

Through meditations on the flora and fauna of his Pennsylvania home, Davis brings readers into a world rife with danger and darkness as well as quietude and splendor. —*Publishers Weekly*

Whether it's the land being ruined, the aging or dying of family and friends, or his own body turning and turning toward what it does, Davis holds his gaze steadily upon it all, gently upon it all, which makes for some mourning, but also plenty of magic. A good deal of sorrow, but even more wonder. —Ross Gay, author of *Catalog of Unabashed Gratitude* and *The Book of Delights*

Davis is unflinchingly candid and enduringly compassionate. —*Harvard Review*

As readers encounter the ordinary miracles that Davis reveals as both father and son within "the kingdom of the ditch," they also are reminded that the human is not apart from nature but a part of it. —*Chicago Tribune*

A poet who has been sure in his voice for decades but has arrived in fullest form. —*Denver Quarterly*

Many poets feel that they know the natural world, but Todd Davis has absorbed this world fully into his heart and mind. He is a fine, rare poet. —Jim Harrison, author of *Legends of the Fall* and *The Shape of the Journey*

A poet with deep knowledge of the land and empathy for his subjects, who delicately and expertly explores how we suffer and pay for our sins, how we can rewild into redemption, and what of this Anthropocene is worth saving. —*North American Review*

He is an immensely talented poet, one of our country's best. —Ron Rash, author of *Serena* and *Something Rich and Strange*

Davis takes in the natural world, from its grand glory down to its microscopic necessity. . . . Underlying all these poems are Davis's unyielding connection to and love for nature. —*Booklist*

Davis's command and keen survey of the outdoors is at once majestically extensive, and disarmingly precise and compassionate. And yet—these nature poems do what most cannot: that in spite of fanciful moments . . . they also serve as a much-needed guidepost and catalyst for wanting to create even more songs of this complicated earth. —Aimee Nezhukumatathil, author of *Oceanic* and *World of Wonders*

Davis gives a resounding and haunting image of what the natural world, and our world, have become. He reminds us that our path is not yet set. —*Southern Review of Books*

In stunning language and elegant prosody, the poet honors life in its great variety. —*Library Journal*

Nouns and verbs have dreams and shadows, as well as their own irreducible essence, and they spill here from the hands of a master. —Rick Bass, author of *For a Little While* and *With Every Great Breath*

Like poets Wendell Berry and Mary Oliver, Davis is committed and spiritually anchored to his home ground, and so the language rises organically from his daily life. —*Orion*

DITCH MEMORY

Books by Todd Davis

POETRY

Coffin Honey

Native Species

Winterkill

In the Kingdom of the Ditch

Household of Water, Moon, and Snow (limited edition chapbook)

The Least of These

Some Heaven

Ripe

ANTHOLOGIES

A Literary Field Guide to Northern Appalachia

Fast Break to Line Break: Poets on the Art of Basketball

Making Poems: Forty Poems with Commentary by the Poets

DITCH MEMORY

NEW & SELECTED POEMS

Todd Davis

with a foreword by David James Duncan

MICHIGAN STATE UNIVERSITY PRESS ■ *East Lansing*

Michigan State University Press
East Lansing, Michigan 48823-5245

LIBRARY OF CONGRESS CATALOGING-IN-PUBLICATION DATA
Names: Davis, Todd F., 1965– author. |
Duncan, David James, writer of foreword.
Title: Ditch memory : new & selected poems /
Todd Davis ; with a foreword by David James Duncan.
Description: First edition. |
East Lansing, Michigan : Michigan State University Press, 2024.
Identifiers: LCCN 2024014999 | ISBN 9781611865110 (cloth) |
ISBN 9781611865103 (paperback) | ISBN 9781609177713 (PDF) |
ISBN 9781628955316 (ePub)
Subjects: LCGFT: Poetry.
Classification: LCC PS3604.A977 D58 2024
LC record available at https://lccn.loc.gov/2024014999

Cover design by Erin Kirk
Cover art by George Boorujy

Visit Michigan State University Press at *www.msupress.org*

For Shelly, Noah & Nathan

Contents

from COFFIN HONEY

from NATIVE SPECIES

from WINTERKILL

from IN THE KINGDOM OF THE DITCH

from THE LEAST OF THESE

from SOME HEAVEN

from RIPE

Foreword: Solaces Gleaned from an Earth Poet's Poem-Stories

David James Duncan

Vote for Goats

One of the first things to surprise me when I began reading Todd Davis's poetry is that, as different as poems and long fiction are as literary forms, Davis's poems are as dedicated to fiction as my novels and short stories. His work teems with stories, some terse, some elaborate, and his books, over time, have become as cohesive as well-wrought novellas. Poet Jane Hirshfield has said of Davis's work, "You can't help but feel that the capacities of human vision, and also our appetite for exactly this way of seeing and naming, have been mysteriously, precisely increased."

I agree, and the modifiers *mysteriously* and *precisely* are exactly right. The narrative points of view in Davis's poems could seem kaleidoscopic at a glance, but look more closely and you find precision, mystery, and clear connection to Earth's natural order in every poem. His work raises unusual questions in me, such as: When an eft stops being an aquatic newt and becomes an Electronic Funds Transfer; when a wind turbine technician is haunted by wild birds who, migrating by stars at night, fly into his tower and are struck as dead as the canaries his coal-miner father closed up in cages to protect himself down in the mines; when the men driving heavy equipment cut a road into the local mountainside, snow piles up all winter, melts in March rain, and the mountain sloughs so much mud and silt down into the creek that its trout all suffocate, hasn't the meaning of the word *Progress* flown from "the progressive development of humankind" to "the penchant of human-unkind to ruin the living world for a paltry paycheck"? When, after Davis's poems had depicted a skein of humans expert in destruction, I met in "Goat Dream" a creature who dreams "a taste in my mouth, a hunger to give thanks for the merciful strength / of jawbone, able to bend metal, to gnash and mince the hardest gourd, // to gnaw the world open and taste what is good," I experienced a political first: a yearning to elect grateful domestic goats to public office instead of the ingrates and cave trolls who govern us now.

Polyphony & Humility

That harmony, counterpoint, polyphony, and musical forms be felt in our work is a desire Todd Davis and I share. Yet, focusing on polyphony, we could hardly be more different. I used multiple narrators in my novels *The River Why*, *The Brothers K*, and *Sun House*, but their voices are all human except for animals briefly borrowed for comic effect. Davis's narrators, in contrast, can be almost anyone or anything, and his polyphonic intent is anything but comic: he is giving voice to the entirety that poet laureate Joy Harjo had in mind when she advised, "Remember the earth whose skin you are." In a brief scan of recent poems, I find Davis giving voice to an epic yet believable black bear named Ursus; to a starving stray dog wandering around a paper mill; to a vernal pond, an underground river, pit ponies jailed for life in coal mines; to the excruciating relationship between a young male rape survivor and a vulture's carcass to whom the boy prays as to a god; to a coffin filled with honey for reasons that shatter the beekeeper who filled it. Davis's arrays of unlikely voices are a stupendous feature of his work, a profligate gift to his readers. To emphasize his ability to leap from point of view to point of view that each tells a story all its own, allow me to reformat Davis's poem "Bear-Eater"—but please read his beautiful original, too:

> The oldest bears, with milky eyes, see through water clearly.
> How easy to catch speckled trout when you follow fins
> between rock folds.

Ten thousand shades of green crowd the understory
while the long history of earth's turning comes to rest
in a bog where white pine stumps rot
like the sawed-off legs of mastodons.

The ancients named the rivers we haven't found yet.
We hide beneath licked limestone, flow for miles
underground.

High in a snag, raven plays priest, croaks
a line about death from the scriptures
written on the creases of corvid brains.

I need to taste my lover's sex
at least once more before I drown.
We should all reenter the slickness
from which we were torn, the blood-soaked
light that ushers us into a body that lasts
such a brief time.

Night's tissue disassembles beneath the line
of the approaching fires we've drawn.
Burning grouse fly ahead of the blaze, illuminate
a path like sparks from an opened furnace door.

It takes the loon so much effort to be skyborne.
Where she took flight, the water churns with small fish,
and heron gullet the slapping bodies until they turn to statues.
This morning, at the confluence of two tributaries,
I washed up on a sandbar and searched for the rookery.

Trees possess the longest memory. They know each of us
who has slept, or eaten, or wept beneath them.

I held the moon last night, pushed my arm into a crater
and brought forth the skeleton of the first bear
who watched over earth's making.

All true, all beautifully envisioned, and the humility of this poet humbles its readers with its limpid honesty. In the poem, "The Last Time My Mother Lay Down with My Father," the same honesty dares to wonder,

> How did he touch my mother's body
> once he knew he was dying? Woods white
> with Juneberry and the question of how
> to kiss the perishing world, where to place
> his arms and accept the gentle washing
> of the flesh.

These lines by the son imbue the father's mortal losses with a clarifying beauty and a sense of immortally healing wonder.

Davis, Ursus & the Good According to Isaac of Syria

I have a close friend in Seattle, a veteran fireman I'll call Seamus to preserve his spiritual secrecy, who has answered roughly twenty thousand alarms in his long career. In a running conversation we've been having for years, I sometimes check in with Seamus on how he deals with the havoc, extreme trauma, and loss of life he witnesses every day. Seamus told me that, early in their careers, he and his firehouse brethren discover a place in themselves from whence they can accept whatever they encounter on an alarm without judging or worrying it. Since fentanyl use became rampant in homeless camps the horrors firemen now witness have become so shocking I can't describe them here. Yet with a steely unity amid which lives are lost and saved daily, Seamus and crew continue to face whatever the crisis demands of them.

As I was working on this foreword, Seamus emailed me to calmly describe, from the previous night, one of the worst human actions I've ever heard of going down in one of the camps. He then followed that horror with one of the most mysterious confessions anyone has ever shared with me. Seamus said, "There is an extra sensibility available if you're paying attention at these scenes." He said, "Amid these bottomless wells of sorrow, the night breeze and birds on nearby branches take on a depth I call *a whispering*." He said, "Angels hover, and everything seems to grow aware." He said, "Even rocks and trees take notice, come alive, pay attention. It's not a case of reality versus imagination. It's as real as the breeze in our hair. And birds especially—something more happens with birds. When I read Jim Harrison's poem about a kid calling birds *holes in heaven*, I knew Jim had sensed the *extra aliveness*, too."

Given the lifetime I've spent pondering wisdom literature, it was a pleasure to search my library for experiences akin to what Seamus had described, and it took me no time to find what I was seeking. In the homilies of the seventh-century Desert Father, Saint Isaac of Syria, he writes: "Be a partaker of the sufferings of all. . . . Rebuke no one, revile no one, not even those who live very wickedly. Spread your cloak over those who fall into sin, each and every one, and shield them." The Firemen's Credo!

But it startled me to then realize that Todd Davis's poems also tap into "an extra sensibility," and refuse to rebuke or revile the evils he sees. In his stunning seventh book, *Coffin Honey*, with Ursus, its mythical old black bear protagonist, I find no poem more illustrative of Saint Isaac's restraint toward those lost in sin than the fourth of four poems titled, "dream elevator." With apologies for condensing Davis's formatting and text, the poem startles by evincing the same signature honesty we find in his poems about natural epiphanies and wonders, but launches with this: "After the man rapes the boy / he climbs the cellar stairs / and walks / into the woods / that border the farm's farthest field. / He smells himself and considers / how sin stains the sinner." No rebuke or reviling by the poet. The sinner is judging himself. Meanwhile the boy, bleeding and weeping, has fetched the key to the gun safe, and armed himself with a shotgun. How sick I am of the murderous American storyline that lies: *Guns make things right*. And how adroitly Davis sidesteps the storyline I'm sick of: "The man stands creek side, / trousers circled / at his feet. Sun clangs on water / as he washes his cock."

Who could possibly absolve this man, spread a cloak over him, shield him from his next sin? Todd Davis knows exactly who, and exactly how: "The sound of water pushing / against stone / masks the bear's approach. / The animal has also smelled the sin and followed his hunger. / The man grasps his own scrotum / and thinks how he could cut away / this part of himself, / leave it to drown in the stream. / He's watched / the boy at mass / as he carries the thurible, ashamed / that he's aroused / by the scent of incense. / Before he can decide / the bear rides the man's head / down against the rocks, / clawing open the chest, / breaking four ribs / and tearing them / from the sternum. / Halfway across the field / the boy hears a scream / and runs."

The nineteenth century's Saint Silouan adds to the seventh century's Saint Isaac, "The man who cries out against evil people but does not lovingly pray for them will never know the grace of God." Davis's poem then ends in that graciousness, Saint Ursus rebuking no one as he lovingly chaws the right ventricle of a disassembled rapist's heart.

Returning to Earth

Though famed for celebrations of the natural world, Davis is just as fascinated by family dynamics, and includes under the heading "family" the human and ecological realms and every species of creature he encounters. Few Americans take our unanimity with the other-than-human more seriously, or more literally—and Davis's literalism is born of science. Douglas Chadwick's seminal book, *Four-Fifths a Grizzly*, is a Davis favorite as it demonstrates that humans and grizzly bears share 80 percent of their DNA; humans and salmon 60 percent; humans and insects 40 percent; and humans and wine grapes 24 percent, unless a good bottle was recently imbibed.

Davis responds to these DNA overlaps in many ways. I, too, resonated with Chadwick's book, but I long ago absorbed its message: Forty years ago my first novel depicted its fisherman protagonist experiencing spiritual rebirth by freeing an epic female chinook salmon after an all-night riverine love scene so much more graphic than the scene between the protagonist and his lovely human partner that every publisher in New York and Boston rejected my novel, only to scratch their heads in confusion when it became a classic that to this day helps pay my bills.

Attention publishers: *Humans are pining for spiritual rebirth*! And the poetry of Todd Davis is providing it. How honored I am to have been invited to speak of the tributaries flowing into a splendid life's work. How skillfully and often tenderly this husband/father/poet continues to live the epigraph for his poem, "Returning to Earth," taken from a line by Czeslaw Milosz: "trust in the light that shines through earthly forms."

NEW POEMS

Midsentence

Water talks slowly, murmurs
its way down the chest
of the mountain, for centuries
licking holes through stone,
beginning to shape the word
bridge, which a fox trots across
only after half the moon
breaks away.

Goat Dream

While I sleep, wind shears the plateau, lifts trees by the crown,
uprooting and felling the oldest or weakest, those sick

with some new blight. Long before we were born, grass tried
to steal from trees. A larger pasture. More wood for the fire. Oaks

and maples. Gray children cloned from the roots of a mother-beech.
Huddling beneath a skirt of branches, they held what now melts:

stumps and snags dripping, windthrows dissolving. Not waste,
as the farmer claims, but a reimagining of what comes after

when we wake. Nothing can separate, not even death as it composts
existence. Like water from the mountain when it enters the river.

A beginning starting with what ended at the tributary's mouth.
Incremental loss, teeth tearing moss, grinding the green passage

of what came earlier. All of it entering the body. Joining me
to snow and rain, to the rocks they cling to. A labyrinth of tunnels.

A warren of roots thick with the memory of chestnut mast.
A red eft navigates the leaf-rubble. A trail to follow. Before I wake

a taste in my mouth, a hunger to give thanks for the merciful strength
of jawbone, able to bend metal, to gnash and mince the hardest gourd,

to gnaw the world open and taste what is good.

The Bear inside the Bear

Within the womb

    of his mother's

        mother's

making,

    the bear inside

the bear wakes

and walks

    the curved space of the world

he inhabits. Her veins

spread

    across the dim red

        sky

like beech limbs

    full of copper

leaf-flutter.

    The world outside

the world

the bear must walk into

changes:

ice melts under blood's thrumming,

snow turns

to rain.

Ursus's mother knows the passage

of time

is mercy,

a prayer of acceptance. She can't help

but hope the men and women

who destroy the world

will be turned

into trees.

Bodies bridged with bark,

arms cleft in contrition.

Chests slashed open

like the canopy

when a tree is thrown

by wind,

sun allowed to fall

into darkness again.

Tributary

I learned to catch the trout's moon whisper.

—HART CRANE

Fish window
water, rise
to bugs
that flock
the air.

Disguised
by limestone
the river worms
underground.

In darkness
on walls
drawings
thousands
of years old:

A bear stands
with arms
reaching
toward
sun.

A bear sleeps
beneath
tamarack
the color
of November.

A bear couples
with her
mate, head
nuzzled
to neck.

In the absence
of light
Ursus squints,
uses a nail
to sketch
the fish
he hopes
to catch.

Like water,
muscle shifts
across time:

The dead
hand
that etched
the first
rock.

A bear's claw
that draws
the trout.

The hidden moon
the trout
whispers to
before
disappearing
into stone.

The Dam on Loup Run

I've begun to dream more and more in the deep
holes of the forest.

Of the men who cut and stacked stone to hold
the water that tumbles the mountain.

Of chestnut trees growing from knee-high stumps
before blight remembers them.

Forgotten by most, the mill's crumbling foundation
reveals how easily we humans can disappear.

Who will consider the speckled trout high up
orphaned from their kin down low?

Ursus knows what it means to be separated, lost
without the one who loved you first.

It's no dream that bears speak through scratched bark.
That's how Ursus learned about the dam.

Out of fear that we'll return, Ursus pries, catches
claws at rough edges, clatters the stony weight.

How often have I thought to wreck this dam?
But that takes courage.

The work's no different than the talus Ursus turns
to follow ants in their spray of confusion.

He hungers for June's touch, to smell the sex of another
and tongue the creased laurel flower.

Stone by stone, the wash of water
opens around him.

In sleep I see fish leap over shoulders, Ursus's head
swinging from side to side.

Some he helps up the remaining ledge,
others he catches with his teeth before they land.

April Prayer

Where snow disappeared a month ago, I trace my fingers

    to wake dirt. In darkness coyotes dragged the carcass

of the doe they'd run down into a tangle of rhododendron.

    If I'm to pray, I must become the thing I pray to: flesh rent,

fur reformed into tufts of hair like the fans my aunts wave

    under their chins in church. My lips scoured

by uninterrupted light, not a single tree leafed out.

    Just words in empty air, for that deer

and those coyotes, for the beauty of the devoured

    and the ones who devour.

For a Stray Dog near the Paper Mill in Tyrone, Pennsylvania

Is that life?—to stand by a river and go.
—WILLIAM STAFFORD

The dog bends her ear to the steel tracks as they begin to hum. Part shepherd part hound, her gait is smooth, and when she trots across the bridge that connects the mountain to the town, she appears to float: each pad-strike pushing air like the broad beat of geese who V the gap of the river. Where water widens and slushes in the slow flow of January, if you look up, you'll see the sky break into pieces around the bridge's rusted arches. The train won't arrive for another few minutes so the dog pauses at the end of the bridge to inspect the abutment. Poured more than a century before, the stone soaks up the curried piss, which like the dog's tracks will wash away in March's meltwaters. She sniffs an abandoned refrigerator, door askew like a broken wing, then trails after deer scent behind a tangled screen of branches. Downriver the clack of the train echoes and multiplies, and near the bend where the paper mill stands, an osprey releases from the top of a snag: bird's sharp cry impossible to hear over the rail squeal that deafens the boy who cups his hands and hollers after a dog with no name.

The Taxidermist's Daughter Retrieves a Head

You smell her, even before you start down
the hollow, rot clotted and beginning to bloat.
She won't rise this year. Body worn by infection,
last days spent septic in the persistent embrace
of hunger. Before the first snow, you watched her.
The odd gait, misshapen paw dragging an awkward line.
What to call a sleep you can't climb out of, a dream
that holds your legs as you try to crawl away?
On this first warm day, you've come for her skull,
to honor her last thoughts by gathering them in the basin
of her bones. You bind a handkerchief across your mouth
and nose and still gag. The hole she crawled through
opens beneath a fallen beech, burrow where light retreats.
You don't mind the dark, having been raised in a house
that looks north. You find her by the rough end of the snout,
draw the great head near, tipping it away from the thick fur
of her chest. After breath is banished, heartbeat
beaten from the body, you live in a room full of death,
walls adorned with skulls. As a child you were taught
to care for carcasses, to salvage roadkill, the dead
dragged back to the barn where the last bit of blood
might drain. The beetles your family keep
in deep plastic bins scramble over flesh, gorging
the residue of past lives. You marvel that they never tire,
desire unfulfilled by the testament of skin and hair.
They tunnel into the ear, ravishing themselves
on the pink folds, eating the sweet meat of memory.
Before exiting her den you feel the rest of her. Thinness
of hips, autumn fat gone. The head slips from your hands
when you bump a lump, dead as well, latched
to a dried breast, mouth still open in protest.

Free Write

The teacher asks the class
to get out their journals.
The girl who sits in the corner
looks out the window.
Like her mother's eyes,
fog droops over the ridges
and makes false promises
about rain. The girl writes,
The sky swirls like a plate
of stones. She writes,
There's a fox skeleton
lodged beneath the bridge
no one knows about.
She draws a picture
of a thrush, scribbles a single
word for its song
and covers it. She thinks,
What's a word as sour
as sheep sorrel's leaf?
She whispers, *Why doesn't*
my tongue shimmer
when it speaks?

Before My Mother's Funeral

Dressed in his preaching suit, raven squawks
about what we're given and what we give
ourselves over to.

The last of the forest churches are being sawn,
toppled to make a thing we can sit on or eat from.

The trees look back at us and see only emptiness.

In turn we dig holes deep in the dirt's chest:
a people of fire burning what will burn.

On her deathbed my mother swore
she heard the Lord God bird knocking.

The proof's in the body, but the coroner
won't open the drawer.

Pit Ponies

Hooves cross the carved history
of horses harnessed to coal carts, forgotten

century orphaned like a corpse. An echo
of a mare's whicker as she's forced to mate

in darkness, offspring birthed from dust
to reshape the world with labor. In this place

a pickaxe strikes the blurred edge of a lantern,
and at midmorning a mud-caked carrot is brought

to searching lips, a pail of blackened water
to relieve a cracked tongue. The rest of the day

nothing but iron's tang on stone, grunts of men
scoring rock to burn. At night in earthen entrails

ponies eat hay scattered in wooden boxes, lick
sweating walls to dull the boredom of thirst.

Moldy straw's the only bed, and sleep's a respite
soiled with fear the lantern's glow won't return.

Always again the calloused hand slapping
a winnowed rump, urging another step.

Eclogue for an Extractive Economy

Each day I think this will be the last
warbler. With the seasons confused
these small birds stay longer and longer
to starve. Wrapped in the long cord
of its vine, I eat a fox grape to darken
my mouth. An itinerant word flees,
a bracelet of language fastened
to the lone deer the neighbor shot
and quartered. Like a white-footed mouse
burrowing beneath snow, the stone in my sister's
body opens to infection. The doctor diagnoses
the shadow and buries it underground
to hold the poison.
                    The geologist also seeks
what's imprisoned. All around us pump jacks
and the sounds of new wells being drilled.
The derrickman ignores what happens
when fossils are dislodged and scattered.
Where the mountain was cut to the ground
there's nothing to hold back the flood.
The last year of his life my father struggled
to breathe. I missed the hour of his death
and woke to blood sopping the pillow.
I pull on my boots before dawn. The elevator
cage clanks as it descends the shaft. Without
much light, it's impossible to see
where the sea used to be.

Silt Psalm

After they sawed the road into the side
of the mountain, snow piled

then disappeared with March rains, water
dragging dirt down, muddying the creek

to a psalm thicker than any song,
drowning speckled trout,

so much silt there was nothing left
to draw breath from.

Fishing with My Seventeen-Year-Old Self

We wade upstream where light marks the passage,
open and forgiving, so when rain begins, wind and thunder
growling over the peak whose base forms the foundation
of this stream, we're more surprised than scared.
A game trail leads us into a willow-thicket, spit of rock
and dirt pushed up by hundred-year floods, a small island
with moving water on all sides, water also moving
from darker skies. Stuffed full of young aspen and alder,
limbs and leaves lay tight as shingles on a roof, and here
in our green hovel, dry and comfortable, we rest, backs
propped on slender trunks, eyes closed, listening
to what now seems far-off weather. The arterial thrush
of the river grows, and when I open my eyes, your face
glistens, faint nimbus exposing the first evidence of moustache
and chin-beard. You're still young enough to sleep anywhere,
and my own old worries have receded as a softer wind
pushes clouds, slivers of sun beginning to unspool
wet branches. A returned warmth hatches flies, and kingfisher
rile the air with their clicking mantra. A bear rustles
willow shoots fifty yards downstream. Rather than wake you
and go back to tempting cutthroat with figured lines, I wait
a bit longer, shelter in this country the same way
I saved leaves to press in a book as a boy.

The Wind Turbine Tech Speaks of Revolutions

Birds migrate at night by stars, then fly into the foreign half-light of my
tower.

Some will be struck by the curves of the propeller.

Harnessed like my great grandaddy's mules, I ascend the hollow pole.

On the best days winds disappear, forest riddled with spiraled shadows
that cut nothing from the sky.

If I fall, I'll be caught up by birdsong echoing through steel.

I'm living my father's life in reverse.

Each morning he packed birds in cages to protect himself when he
wandered into the earth.

Some perished when tunnels collapsed; others, nestled among coal
heaps, struggled to catch a last breath.

Up here I scramble toward sun to steal invisible air.

Mine is a day of slow revolutions.

After the Elk Hunt

She straddles him the same way he straddled
the bull while gutting the animal two days before,
stealing what lived inside to eat the rest
of the year. Strong from walking angled ridges,
her thighs squeeze his ribs to a fine point
where pain passes like heat from a wood stove's
open door. Each of us, animals that we are,
possess a cortex that folds: furrowed messages
stored in a black room, curtains parted
to the fracturing light of another's touch.
As he bends upward toward her throat,
he's washed in the smell of the creek
she bathes in, and she, stretching into his chest,
by the tang of the carrots he pulls from the dark
soil in the garden. They share the memory
of quick inhalation as the bullet pierces
a lung, blood strung on ground where it exits.
Now as his cartilage shifts with her pleasure,
their rough tongues search for water
in each other. She follows the muscle
along his spine with her fingers, recalling
the animal's backstrap as it hung from a spruce
branch, body still in need of quartering.
Together, this first night after they pack out
the meat, their own flesh creased by the antlers
they strapped to their bodies, they trace
indentations, gullies that will slowly fill
over the next week as new blood pumps
beneath skin. Long ago they were taught
by their parents to eat the heart, sliced
thin and braised in butter. Woodfire
lights their greasy fingers as they hold

a piece of what propelled the hooves
forward, even after death had been decided.
Somewhere in the dark the last divots
mark mud and grass, and a late meadow
fritillary beats its wings among seed heads
with the tenderness of parted lips.

Of This Failing

Because I chase trout
up the mountain,
an abacus of fish teeth
scar my finger.

High in a tree
the sun sticks to pine sap,
a poultice for the ring
the porcupine teethes.

After a full circle
of moons,
the delicious
degradation
of the spawn.

Where our son's head
crowned, you draw me
into the dark sphere
that closes the ground.

You whisper
that years from now
a hairy woodpecker
will drill down
through the scar
to collect
a grub's memory
of this failing
afternoon light.

Vernal Pond

In this earthen bowl

           where snows

    have melted,

sacks

       of frog eggs

   drift.

You wrote

    yesterday

       to report

on the test:

    brain scan
           in a lonely

white tube,

    someone shining

        a light

in your eyes.

       Spring peepers

drown the traffic

from the road below.

The wind

sways moosewood

branches,
a clacking sound

like the machine
that looked inside

your skull.

You know all of this,

having studied

wetlands.

The egg-sacks float

like ships caught in doldrums.

The report says

you have Alzheimer's.

By the end

of June

these waters will be gone.

Sitting near the pond

I regret

that so much of the world

must disappear.

Apostate

Beneath a new moon I enter the vast and stoneless field,
feet bared to tilled soil where the very first rocks should be,
those stones who cried out and allowed trees to sprout
between them, roots holding. This was before the coming
of my grandfather and his grandfather who cleared a footpath
in the forest, a field owned and increasing on either side
of the path, which now is a road, and in that field with each plowing
stones unearthed, dragged to the far side with the help
of horses and mules, oxen oaring the weight of a stoneboat,
and there stacked, resting one upon another, exposed
as if in warning, no longer warmed by earth and now named *wall*,
and I do not know how long it will take to undo this doing,
but I begin with a single stone, carrying it to the field's center,
and there, like a seed, burying, then gathering another, disassembling
that wall, weight burning my back, planting rock after rock,
making impossible the plow's work, and with the aid of vireo
and thrush, warbler and wren, with the mouths and bowels
of so many animals, who just by eating and shitting plant
a new world: fences brought down, barriers returned to earth,
furrows forgotten, and a forest I will never see
already growing.

Reservoir/Crows/Climate Change

A day will no doubt come when dust flies at the bottom of seas,
and how can mountaintops avoid the transformation to gravel?
—PO CHÜ-I

No one remembers a time so dry.
Skeletons rise from the lake's disappearing

center and trees that drowned a hundred years before
crawl toward shore. Where three crows dip

and swim, the sky empties. Three more appear
in stagnate reflection, fixed to black water.

Six wavering shadows that squawk and croak
search through the blue rubble of this crumbling

mountain, which soon will turn to fire,
then gravel, then dust.

The Doctor Asks My Friend to Follow the Light at the End of Her Pen

Just past daylight the first morning of deer season, the fingers on his left hand go numb. The second time he passes out we're still half a mile from the truck. He's a large man and takes up most of the backseat where I've covered him in old newspapers and blankets. At the hospital, he opens his eyes to what he describes as a fence of bones: head at rest in the deer's chest. At 84 his grandmother's stroke pinned her to the bed. She said ginseng grew in clusters around her feet and she needed to dig the root to heal. Of all of us on the mountain, he's the best tracker. I've seen him get on all fours and follow a trail into a thicket of multiflora rose. As his eyes track the pen, a heron glides above a thin line of shinning water. He smells spoiled eggs and thinks of the swamp where he saw the largest snapping turtle of his life bury itself beneath a log. The gray bird slowly beats its wings toward the horizon while the monitor hooked to his arm buzzes like a woodcock. The doctor's pen moves back and forth. My friend's eyes stay snagged on a branch.

At Last I Can Understand What the Birds Are Saying

I slip

    between

stones

    where water

enters

    the world

from beneath

      stone

and cools

      air

flirting

    with

    warblers

and thrushes

    who hide

their songs

with leaves

and small trout

secreted

under

sunken logs

growing

accustomed

to my body

beginning

to race

along

my sides

fins like feathers

as if

wind

caught me

                    up

over
            the canopy

showing me

            how we

are always

                    leaving

the earth
                            so

            at last

I
            can understand

what the birds

                    are saying

Wayfaring

In winter the titmouse sings
Peter, Peter, Peter,
renaming me for the story
I've been told and now
must tell.

Six days before solstice
we sleep late, wake
to a darkness we know
will grow.

Do all moments grieve
the passing of the last?

The frame on my mother's dresser
holds a photo of a turtlehead
flower found creekside
in late summer: green stalk
and milky petals, a blossom
like a mouth gasping for breath.

What prayer do we answer
in living for another?

Time with you, my love,
slips like water from an eddy:
counterclockwise swirl
that foams past a fallen beech
set crossways in a stream.

My fingers fan air, release the ash
of loved ones, a cloud over
the place where the river
we fish in the valley
begins.

If my hand offends me,
I will befriend it, the reason
I hold the brook trout tenderly,
tangerine belly squirming
from my grasp.

When my father said,
God beats in our chest,
did he mean God lives
in our heart or simply
chooses to wreck it?

River voices are always
tempting me from beneath
the bridge. Would it be a sin
to tumble and become one
with the wash?

December light weighs
next to nothing: faint shimmer
like a bead of oil
in a flame-blackened pan.

It was April before you died,
a blood clot circling
your brain.

In the coldest months
the river slushes, slow,
furtive movements,
like your drooping eye,
the useless fingers
of your left hand.

This past October
we watched a storm-blown
tanager lose its way in migration.
That night I gave thanks
for the map of blue veins
in your breasts.

I've decided if my eye
causes me to sin, rather than
pluck it out, I'll simply close it.

Stars waver in the dark, glistening
like dew on dimpled berries.

In your absence I repeat
the names of trees you taught me:
hop hornbeam and catalpa, syllables
like rain on a tin roof.

At this early hour, I still haven't
heard a cock crow.
Like Peter, I've denied
the truth three times.

Fishing with Nightcrawlers

From the bank beneath a basswood, I fling a nightcrawler
for my sons, too small to cast for themselves. The bait drifts
with the current, and I pass the rod to the oldest one, my own
hands secretly holding from below. You were a boy in this town
along the South Skunk River. I wonder if you carried your pole
over your left or right shoulder, if the worms you dug in the backyard,
squirming as you lowered them over the hook, smelled on your fingers
when you handed the bluegill you caught to your mother, the stringer
clanking against the sink's enamel basin. Her fingers filmed over
as she dunked the meat in egg and milk, rolled the pink flesh
in breadcrumbs, the kitchen hazy with burnt butter, as if a boy
in vestments had trailed by the table swinging a censer, how you
peered through the hole made by her elbow and waist, hoping
there'd be enough white bread to sop up the blackened grease.

Bare Limbs

All night and into morning
we hear the apples dropping.

Hundreds of them. Thump
of bodies as they hit

the ground. More apples
in a single season than all the years

since we planted the seedlings.
This past spring, a year after

the worst drought on record,
blossoms begged the air.

All for the sake of propagation.
A continuance. Just six days since

a dear friend was finally shaken
to death by Parkinson's. We wake

to bare limbs. I gather and peel
another bushel while Shelly slices

the meat and pours lemon juice
to keep the flesh from turning.

Despite these last warm days,
we fire the oven to make cobbler,

flame the stove to boil sauce. A bit
of extra sugar to soothe the sour bite.

This Shared Life

These last thirteen years
I've eaten your body.
Your only son,
I think you'd be happy
how you've become
the tart sweetness
of huckleberry that darkens
my oatmeal.

And now,
in November,
with the tamaracks
glowing, a part of you
low to the ground
rounds into the shape
of red teaberries
whose mint opens
to my teeth.

Overhead vultures tilt,
shimmering an ashy
incandescence,
filtering down
to where those
who love me
will someday lay me
next to you.

And in that
not-too-far-off June,
among those ten
thousand bushes,
flowers will bloom
out of us, and by July
with joy my sons
will roll a ripe
mouthful of berries
over their tongues.

Deposition: What Was Lost

I follow light across pine

                needles

      where a fox pads over

                the first hours

      of my mother's dying.

At the table

      a glass of juice,

      a glass of water,

                a cup

      of coffee gone cold.

Each a shadow

      that crawls the sweating surface

of my skin.

                I think

          of the clothesline

      in the yard,

                    thin

rope
                    of smoke

in the air.

                        I think

of the fox's tail,

                        how it waves a warning

        or curls in fear.

                        When I find the burrow

        and hear kits mewling,

I think of my sister

                        at the bee boxes.

        A photo

where she holds the lid

        with a grin,

                        cuts the comb,

the way I was cut

from our mother's womb:

honey

with melted butter on bread

still warm from the oven.

Last Baptism

I'll tell a portion
of that child:
bones of the skull
yet to knit, soft
skin of delicate
legs draped
on my arm,
the winged
flutter
when the water
splashed,
parents smiling
nervously
as I laid an ear
to the child's
chest to hear
the beating,
the same
I'd done
to every dog
I'd owned,
to the cat
who sleeps
in the crook
of my legs,
and long ago
on the family
farm, to sheep,
to goats, to mules
my father
plowed with,
the donkey

my mother bonneted,
a raccoon
my brother raised
from a kit, even
a mouse
I trapped
beneath a box
to carry outside
for my mother,
who killed nothing
she didn't eat,
and while I'd
momentarily
stunned
the mouse,
chasing it
with a broom,
I heard inside
that slight chest
a thumping
that helped me
believe
in the quickening,
God touching
this flesh we find
ourselves in,
and so I said
to that child
in the church
of my hands
as she gulped air,
water having shocked

the heart, shocking
the congregation, too,
"Remember
pick up the bone
from your plate,
slurp the orange
grease from fingers,
put an ear to the chest
of those you love,
laying cheek to breast,
because sometimes
life can be tender
and supple, as giving
and forgiving
as the pink
of a nipple."

A Friend Writes to Tell Me How Hildegard of Bingen Cried Viriditas!

A shoe thrown, an axle broken
by stone. The horse plods on

searching for a creek
to drink from.

Doesn't the wood of the violin,
even when splintered,

remember the first notes played?
Stars descend through ascending

smoke. Two mountains removed
the green flames of the first summer

fires glow. We're downwind
in the dark, downriver swimming

naked. Your hand on my back,
mine reaching for your front.

The god of light still
hours away.

Ditch Memory

I had in mind the wagon road
that crosses the back field
where the ivory flowers
of wild carrot wash
over the banks.

from COFFIN HONEY

Buck Day

Downstairs her mom cooks eggs and deer steaks,
pours coffee in the bottom of a cup clouded
with milk and sugar.

Outside her dad talks about a buck on his trail camera,
steam rising from mouth, a reminder of the spirits
that drift up from storm drains in winter.

Her boyfriend works for the township. Like a blood clot
moving through a vein, he walks miles beneath streets
in tunnels of pipe.

She looks forward to these gray days: to sitting quietly
and saying nothing, to absorbing the cold. In the stand,
her shoulder rests against her dad. She lays the rifle, precise
as a ruler, across her lap.

During sophomore year, when she cut herself,
she used a razor in the bathtub. The water blurred red
lines, like a story with no end.

The moon's nearly faded. Her dad nudges her.
Forty yards away a doe and spike figure-eight the field.
He whispers, "Yearlings," says they'll be tender.

On Sunday the minister proclaimed
no one could gaze upon the face of God.
She wonders what the eyes or nose might reveal,
if the burning bush stank like the lamb Adam roasted
on a spit after he was kicked out of the garden.

It's been two years since she stopped cutting.
She rubs Vaseline where the skin knit unevenly,
but pink ridges remain.

She likes the taste of meat but hopes they'll keep running.
Her dad won't let her shoot at a moving deer.

The doe doesn't stop, but the spike falters, halts and bends,
mouth tugging at a fern.

She squeezes the trigger.

On the felt board outside Sunday school, Jesus waits
for Roman soldiers to nail him to the cross.

Her dad smiles as they walk to the animal, says,
"Now the real work," and hands her the knife.

Like field goal posts, the dead buck's legs splay.
She scores the belly and lets the blade run up
the chest, careful not to nick the intestines.

Thomas doubted until he reached his hand into Jesus's side.
With the deer's chest gaping, she touches the trachea
and lungs, imagines the deer opening its mouth to breathe.

It's easy to get lost in the body's house. That's why
she carved openings in her skin.

She cuts away the deer's heart, gives it to her dad,
who slides the warm meat into a plastic bag
where blood, still pooled in one of the chambers,
begins to leak out.

What I Know about the Last Lynching
in Jeff Davis County

How it happened more than fifty years before I was born. How nobody
in our family talks about it. How I learned in history class that white
people strung up black people. How my cousin Mary Lou has dark
skin because my uncle's brown as hemlock bark. How some still don't
take kindly to my mom's sister marrying the way she did. How Mary
Lou and me listen for the sound of water on the mountain and follow
it under rhododendron. How our history teacher was suspended by
the school board for saying blacks still get lynched when police choke
them. How we catch and split speckled trout. How my uncle taught us
this. How when we go to Dollar General for worms, a clerk trails Mary
Lou up and down each row while I steal gum and two jawbreakers.
How the orange wound of the fish's skin reveals the sweet pink we fry
in butter and salt. How the dad of our best friend has a confederate flag
on his truck's back window. How when we suck on the jawbreakers, our
tongues and teeth turn blue and red. How my uncle won't go into the
bar on Main Street. How some say that black man had to die on the tree
because he whistled at a white woman. How me and Mary Lou made
a book about it. How my uncle still says *Yes sir* to every white man he
speaks to. How Mary Lou can draw near anything. How once she made
a picture of a black and white warbler that's taped to the back of my
bedroom door. How we never showed anyone that book. How I wrote
the story so the man could come back to life like Jesus. How my uncle
taught us to whistle like that bird. How we buried the book in a tin box
in the woods. How we still use that whistle to warn if someone's coming.
How I worry about my uncle when I think of our best friend's dad. How
Mary Lou drew other black men cutting the man down from the tree.
How the tree understood the man would miss the soft skin on the back
of his daughter's arms. How Mary Lou says the bird is striped like prison
bars. How the oak is rotting from a fungus now. How the branches keep
breaking off.

Ursus in the Underworld

For everything that rises must converge.
—PIERRE TEILHARD DE CHARDIN

Plott hounds scramble the tunnel's rock, yowling
and scenting Ursus's shadow. They're devoured
by the dark the deeper they go. Their masters
who have trained them won't descend, having chased
the bear the better part of the day. They build a fire
at the entrance to wait and consider the small extinctions
of the self, outlined in a string of tobacco spit.
Running downward beneath the earth's ceiling
exposes the frailty of light, and in the underworld,
where dreams reside, Ursus finds evidence
that bear have lived since before the foundation
of the world: Callisto searing the sky with Ursus's name,
her child Arcas joining her. Everything that rises
must converge, but over a lifetime hounds will fight
and rifles bark fire that blisters bone. For years the skeleton
of Ursus's mother lay uncovered on a talus slope
where during a summer storm she was struck by lightning.
The flame transformed bits of memory into a bone-pyre.
Beneath the moon and stars, the beacon burned like a dog's
beautiful baying. Now the ridge above Monture is mostly ash,
and deep in its sooty stomach, where the dogs corner Ursus,
the transmitters that ring the Plotts' necks fail, leaving silence
in the empty hands of the waiting hunters. Hades wore the head
of a bear as he chased Persephone: lust being the work we do
in death as in life. Out of this underworld the green
luminescence of the first dog's eyes is birthed, wisest
of hounds who recognizes the bear as the messenger of death.
It climbs out of the blackness, captured in a flashlight's halo,
head poking from one of the crudely dug air vents,
covered in coal dust and blood, ear torn
where Ursus tried to whisper his secret

Coffin Honey

I.

Bees dying.

In hive.

Beneath petals.

Among engineered

leaves and blades,

the zippered pods

of glistening beans.

A chemical sun

showering kernelled light.

II.

The beekeeper raises a bee-box lid,

scrapes bodies

from comb, wax filling

behind fingernails,

embalmed

in stickiness.

III.

Honey made by the dead
is sweet.

The dead floating in honey
makes a daughter weep.

IV.

Fingers to lips.

     Fingers to tongue.

          Tongue crossing teeth.

               A boat ferrying the dead.

                    Traversing the river

                         of our mouths.

V.

Fingerprints:

      whirls

of deceit

      left

on whatever

      we

beseech.

VI.

The beekeeper's daughter searches for survivors.
Surveys the forest canopy for remaining swarms
to gather and take back to her father.

At the end of a branch, she finds striped bodies
crawling over one another, swaying in air, a sound
like her mother's as the tumor consumed her.

VII.

The first time she's stung

                        she jumps,

screams,

                runs out

into a clover-drenched

                                field

where she thinks

        she's safe.

VIII.

A face made of bees

        flies to the edge

of the woods, hovers

        there, turns and shakes

its head

                in disapproval.

IX.

As lungs fill,
she hears
a buzzing inside
her.

As if she's
a bee flying
to the center
of the hive.

    X.

The beekeeper

       finds

the body

       in tall grass,

green and shaking

       with wind:

       puffed

with welts,

       purpled

from loss

     of oxygen,

cankered

red

     from the shock

of trying

     to help.

XI.

In the cool of the cellar,
in the dim light

just beneath the lip
of the earth,

he builds a small box,
five feet by three, milled

less than a month before
from a beetle-infested pine.

XII.

The beekeeper smothers
                   the girl

        in streams
            of honey,

           only her front

teeth
        showing,
           the same

as when she suckled

           her mother,
           and after

her mother's
        death,

           her thumb.

XIII.

The stink of earth
           opened.

XIV.

Scratch of shovel
        and pick.

Repetition of ruin.

Hands keeping time
        with the clang.

XV.

Late at night, drunk on mead,
the beekeeper recites the story
of a body fed only honey:

        How the girl who ate
        amber for each meal
        smelled of clover

and goldenrod,

        how she shined

like a thousand sunflowers

        looking directly

        into the sun.

Possum

In deep summer, when the creek dries up,
copperheads stir like water on limestone, ripples
that steal a gaze and stay you in place. The crossbands
on their backs, like hourglasses, run down to death.
Daddy carries a .22, shoots near anything that moves.
When he was a child, a sister lost part of an arm to venom.
Gangrene crawling like a colicky baby toward her breast.
Bone saw was the only thing to arrest it. Mamaw claims
a nick in the moon ushers in mating, musk like cucumbers
in the garden. I found my snake-killer riding the back
of his dead mother in the red gravel along the road.
Nose like a pink flower sticking up through matted fur.
I don't know what happened to his brothers. Didn't check
the pouch. It was no secret what the tire did. I picked him up
like a sack of millet. He bared his teeth. Tiny opposable
thumbs clamped to my fuck-you finger. Don't kill a possum.
They'll murder copperheads for you. Clear snakes
from stonewalls. Usher the dead from under squash
and pumpkin leaves. You should see him sit up
and take notice when I dangle a gizzard over his craw.
You'd swear a smile wrinkles that sour face.

Field Sermon

*Men are not where he is / Exactly now, but they are around
him / around him like the strength / Of fields.*
—JAMES DICKEY

Walking the mile through blossoming laurel to church,
the preacher wallows clay banks along the river, wailing

a song with furrows. He wants to remember this place
when he stands at the altar, slicked red, barefoot tracks

across the pine floor. He'll chastise what's left
of the congregation for not having faith that corn

will sprout, pole beans plump and wrapped around the legs
of a trellis. Vultures circle a month with no rain,

and a voice swings from the belly, like the stump chains
he uses to drag trees from the woodlot. Raphael and Azrael,

the mules he named after reading the Book of Revelation,
bear the weight, and slowly the field reveals itself in unfolding

absence. As if they were in the presence of an archangel,
trees buckle and kneel, and he hauls them on a skid of words:

salvation, repentance, sin, a backward formula he believes in.
Like a tick at the edge of a dog's ear, his face bloats

when he shouts *grace*, a puzzle as convoluted as wild carrot's
lace, dangerous as hogweed's sap. He loves the story of the man

blinded by it, struck down like Paul near Damascus, arcing
a scythe to the base of the stalk, umbrella of flowers

causing boils to rise from his arms and scales to scar his eyes.
He believes God asks us to suffer as Christ suffered, thorns

biting the skull, sin's venom veining its way to the heart.
When he castrates the hogs in spring, he hollers a line

from Leviticus, knowing how he loves the pink fat,
thanking Jesus he can fry it in a pan without retribution.

When his voice grows raspy, a rusted hinge in need of mercy,
he holds out his hands like a tin cup to where the seep streams

from a cleft in the rock. Thirst slaked, a piece of jerky hangs
like a rat's tail from the corner of his mouth. This past fall

he set aside two ewes, choosing not to breed them.
The ram horn-smashed every fence and gate, a victim

of interrupted lust. The preacher culled the beast, slaughtered
and ground into sausage. He knows even the beloved

will be tempted, and temptation is an empty corncrib,
milking cow butchered for meat, children left with no milk

to drink. All around him hushed *Amen*s echo from hemlock limbs,
the fevered *Hallelujah*s of a poplar careen like a logging truck

near a bend. He lifts his arms to the sky and asks the newly
cleared field, *Brother, who is your true lover? Sister,*

in whose bed do you lie at night? As if in answer, he hears rattles
before he sees the den of snakes gathered in the root-space

left by a beech. This ball of serpents tangles with what he's
convinced are the demands of faith. God is with him,

or the morning cool enough to have dulled the rattlers,
so when he picks one it doesn't strike, allows him to stroke

its ridged skin, to drape it like a preaching scarf around his neck.
Seduction of coils caressing the throat as he whispers a prayer

and kneels in sunlit soil. The fang's sting isn't so different
from what he feels when he tends his bees, but shock slithers out

like a snake's tongue, slurs his speech, as if he's been taken
by the Spirit: a babble over turned earth.

Taxidermy: Cathartes aura

When the vulture fell
from the sky, the boy gathered
the outstretched wings and folded
the body to his breast, feathers
cresting his shoulder, a span
of plumage for riding thermals,
drifting ever higher
above the earth.

The bird's spiraling descent
was unexpected like when
his uncle touched him
in the cellar as he shoveled
coal for winter, telling him
he couldn't have the fried
doughnuts sprinkled
with confectioner's sugar
if he screamed
or told his mother.

Over the next week
the boy slit the dead bird
from neck to tail feathers,
pulled out what had grown inside,
and used cornstarch to dry
the wet residue. He wished to keep
some semblance of the bird
alive before the memory
migrated and was forgotten.

His uncle's white whiskers
stung his cheeks, coffee-breath
at his ear demanding he remove
his pants and later wash
the blood-soaked underwear
at the sink in the garage.

While he worked, tears fell
into the dark space
he'd opened to insert
wires beneath the wings,
around the fragile ribs.
It hurt to sit and burned
when he bore down, excrement
swirled red in the toilet.

In the days that followed
his uncle wanted more,
but the boy begged,
and the man made him take it
in the mouth instead.

He woke with decay in his nostrils
and tried to figure the nature
of the bird's death, but found no bullet
or pebbled buckshot, no evidence
to explain any of this.

He assumed it would go on
until he was older, big enough
to drive a fist into his uncle's throat,
or for that man to keel over,
heart given out while skinning
a raccoon he'd trapped
or turning sod in the garden.

The boy believed the bird
had become the thing
it coveted, having consumed
so much dead flesh, and he stuffed
the cavity with rags and cotton,
sewed the incision and dangled it
with fishing-line over his bed.

Each night before he closed his eyes,
he stared at the pink head, the only
resurrection he believed in now,
and when his mother extinguished
the hall light, he prayed
to the shadow that hung above
to show him how to take flight.

dream elevator

The blood will be a sign for you on the houses where you are,
and when I see the blood, I will pass over you.
—EXODUS 12:13

After the man rapes the boy .

        he climbs the cellar stairs

and walks

        into the woods

     that border the farm's farthest field.

He smells himself and considers

               how sin stains the sinner.

The boy cries in a corner

     of the cellar, remembering

       three crows

who drank from the pond.

           Blood smears his jeans,

    and he crawls

up the steps,

      goes to the bureau in the bedroom

where the key

to the gun safe is kept.

The man stands creek side,

trousers circled

at his feet. Sun clangs on water

as he washes his cock,

balls shriveled in the April cold.

Exposed and weak,

like the stalk of a fern,

the boy lifts the shotgun

from the rack. His shoulders shake

as he sights the barrel.

His father taught him to exhale

before pulling the trigger.

This past November he shot a deer

and steam rose from the gut pile:

lungs and intestines like an altar.

                                        The sound of water pushing

                against stone

                        masks the bear's approach.

        The animal has also smelled the sin

and followed his hunger.

                                        The man grasps his own scrotum

                and thinks how he could cut away

                        this part of himself,

leave it to drown in the stream.

                He's watched

                                        the boy at mass

as he carries the thurible, ashamed

                        that he's aroused

                by the scent of incense.

                                        Before he can decide

the bear rides the man's head

      down against the rocks,

clawing open the chest,

               breaking four ribs

     and tearing them

          from the sternum.

Halfway across the field

     the boy hears a scream

          and runs.

What he sees is a body

     that looks like a broken

vase.

               Purple and white

       flowers cling to the rim

of the wound,

          and the slick petals

     of that damnable

            heart

rankle

            as Ursus chews

the right ventricle.

Mother

After the animal that drank sound died, the world
lay still and cold for months.
—WILLIAM STAFFORD

She drank sorrow, bringing my face
to her neck. She drank the kingfisher's
clicking, pileated's knocking. She drank
the clatter the creek makes when it rains.
She drank frost heaves, widowmakers
descending in wind. She chewed leafduff
scratched away by the flowering of polygala
and violet. She lapped at the dark
cries of coyote and barred owl, rabbit
bleats devoured. Before wings disappeared,
she opened her mouth to the erratic
flight of bats. When I fell from the tree,
she drank the wound on my back, spooned
the sound of a rat snake eating mice
beneath the porch. She loved cricket chirp,
the metal of cicada scritch-scritching.
She swallowed the stomp of mules, the snarl
of dogs. She said the red moon, rocketing
the sky, was like kerosene on kindling,
a fire to illuminate our insides. I asked how
a river buries itself when it dies.
She laughed and drank the weariness
of such questions. I need to be more
careful, to listen intently and learn
to drink better. It's been months
since I conjured her voice.

Bear-Eater

Now there are bear dreams again for the bear-eater.
—JIM HARRISON

After I ate the warm heart of the bear, I slept,
and when I woke, a bobcat eyed my lips, my red fingers
gripping the emptied purse.

A hunger flutters the skull like a swallowtail bumping
against the boned dome of sky.

The oldest bears, with milky eyes, see through water clearly.

How easy to catch speckled trout when you follow fins
between rock folds.

Ten thousand shades of green crowd the understory
while the long history of earth's turning comes to rest
in a bog where white pine stumps rot
like the sawed-off legs of mastodons.

The ancients named the rivers we haven't found yet.

We hide beneath licked limestone, flow for miles
underground.

I worry about when the next cubs will be born.
How we might go on, you and I, this species
we've become.

To clear my head I drink from a small spring,
settle into a patch of sunlight emptied
by dead ash trees.

We mustn't forget to listen
for the faint singing
that drifts up through the cracks
in the streambed.

High in a snag, raven plays priest, croaks
a line about death from the scriptures
written on the creases of corvid brains.

Just now I don't want another death song.

I need to taste my lover's sex
at least once more before I drown.

We should all reenter the slickness
from which we were torn, the blood-soaked
light that ushers us into a body that lasts
such a brief time.

Night's tissue disassembles beneath the line
of the approaching fires we've drawn.

Burning grouse fly ahead of the blaze, illuminate
a path like sparks from an opened furnace door.

It takes the loon so much effort to be skyborne.
Where she took flight, the water churns with small fish,
and heron gullet the slapping bodies until they turn to statues.

This morning, at the confluence of two tributaries,
I washed up on a sandbar and searched for the rookery.

Begging for one more raven prophecy, coyote tracks
ran me in circles, and I lost any sense of direction.

Trees possess the longest memory. They know each of us
who has slept, or eaten, or wept beneath them.

I held the moon last night, pushed my arm into a crater
and brought forth the skeleton of the first bear
who watched over earth's making.

Until Darkness Comes

A 100-year-old gray and ductile iron foundry in Somerset, PA,
has issued a closing notice to workers, according to local reports.

The white blades turn the sky: red-
eyed turbines blinking away the danger
of flying things. Small children float up
over the Alleghenies, parents chasing
the dangling ropes of weather balloons.
It's hard to predict when a storm may blow through.
A boy huddles by a bedroom window, wonders
if his father knows where every deer hides
on the mountain. It's his job to pull the sled
when his father makes a kill. He's been taught
in school the wind that circles the blades carries
electricity to the towns where steel was made.
Three years ago his sister disappeared in the clouds,
heat lightning like veins in the sky. She sends a letter
once a month with a weather report and money
their mother uses for an inhaler. Most of the coal dust
has settled, but fires burn on the drilling platforms
and the prehistoric gas smells like the eggs that spoil
in the hutch when the hens hide them.
The boy never wants to leave this place.
Everything important is buried here: his grandparents,
a pocket knife he stole from his best friend, the eye-teeth
of an elk he found poached at the bottom of a ravine.
Yesterday in the barn a carpenter ant drilled a hole.
The boy bent to the sawed-circle and blew into it,
breath forced down into darkness. He dreams each night
of a horse galloping from a barn, mane on fire
like a shooting star. He prays for a coat sewn from pigeon
feathers, for small wings to fly over the tops of trees
where the children land when their balloons begin to wilt.
On summer evenings barn swallows career like drones,

gorging dragonflies that skim the swamp.
The birds' blue shoulders cant and angle, breast
the color of the foundry's smokestacks as they crumble
beneath wrecking balls and bulldozers, extinguishing
the mill fires the boy's grandfather never dreamt
would go out.

In the Garden

When the last pollinator fluttered its wings and folded
into itself, like newspaper as it catches flame,
we'd already buried the skeletons of the remaining
hummingbirds, the husks of bees, what little was left
of the antennae of moths and butterflies, the tiny corpses
of the penultimate wasp and ant, the sting and bite
of these small lives no longer a threat. Nothing had to be done
for the scurrying beetles who burrowed into caskets
of their own making, but some of us hung the now still
bodies of swerving bats from lampposts, while others gathered
them in nets, making pilgrimages to caves to lay them to rest.
At a museum in Washington, DC, small brass plates named
each creature, explained their place in the vanishing taxonomy.
Underground installations housed seeds for plants and trees,
and we collected an example of each species
that played a role in fertilization, pinned them to a board
with elaborate charts that identified body parts
and their peculiar uses. We were most interested in
their mechanical efficiency and wished to recover
the ways they conveyed pollen from anther to stigma.
We brought in theologians who revised the sign of the cross,
a version that emphasized reproductive organs
and the importance of fecundity. Even the scientists believed
resurrection, grown in a Petri dish, was our only chance:
stigmata marking the wings of a swallowtail or monarch,
each of us longing to touch the holes we'd help to make
in the colorful fabric. This was our prayer to unburden us
of doubt, and despite our lack of faith, we ached for a peach
at the end of a branch, a plum or apple, the honeyed pears
we greedily ate in August, juice dribbling from our chins,
fingers sticky with our own undoing. The few scientists
who were not already living off-planet began to create

new designs for our children's hands and lips,
working to enhance the ridges in the brain that help
to discern and process olfactory signals. They wrote code
while the future slept in its fleshly rooms, reprogramming
the cells for stunted growth, perfectly proportioned
for the work that lay ahead. Where some might have seen
deformity, we saw beauty: sons and daughters walking
orchard rows, crawling between cornstalks and vineyard grapes,
scaling almond trees whose cupped blossoms waited to be filled
with our answers. The children stopped at each bloom,
stooped with fingers shaped like paintbrushes, caressing
silky petals as grains of pollen caught against their skin,
enough static so this precious dusting wouldn't fall away,
until they delivered it to a flower of our choosing.

Sitting Shiva

If you find the bones of a bear, sit down and stay with them.
The dead desire our company. Touch each one—scapula,
tibia, ulna—even the tiniest bones of the hind and forefeet,
the curve of every claw. Just out of sight, a thrush will sing.
Bird song is a way to speak in secret. Find comfort
in the arbutus that whitens each March on the old logging road.
Wait until dark. A full moon will rise from the bear's skull,
showing what she thought of us. Hold the moon-skull in your lap,

stroke the cranial ridges. You may see your dead father
scaling the talus to the blueberry field where this bear ate,
mouth sated and purpled by the sweetest fruit. Your mother
will be in the room on the second floor of the house, packing
and then unpacking a box of your father's clothes. It's hard
to give up this life. But we must. Others are waiting behind us.

from NATIVE SPECIES

Almanac of Faithful Negotiations

Here, at the edge of heaven,
I inhabit my absence.
—TU FU

On the first day, we find evidence of elk but not the elk themselves.

On the second, we see the charred and blackened sleeves fire leaves but not a single flame.

By the third day, the oldest trees have already ascended but the microbial mouths buried in the dirt remain.

After four days, our minds flood with rivers and creeks, and we find it hard to speak, except in mud and stone.

On the fifth, ravens decorate a white-oak snag, croaking in the voices of our drunk uncles, reminding us whose house we live in.

Six days gone, a fisher stands on hind legs, stares across the meadow's expanse, dares us to approach the porcupine-corpse, muzzle red with the body's sugar.

When the last day comes, only minutes before dawn, susurration of wind, stars moving back into the invisible, all of us wondering when we will join them.

Decadence

If the ancients deny heaven treasures wine, *and say*
moon has never understood wine—*I know it's nonsense.*
—YANG WAN-LI

A fawn, no older than four days, wobbles
          to stand beneath her mother's belly, bumps
her still-forming head against the udder,
          which starts the flow of milk. The delicious
sweetness of dame's rocket, pink and purpled,
          fills the air and makes me think this is what the fat
in doe's milk tastes like as it seeps
          from her nipples into the slurping mouth
of her young. The month of May possesses
          a viscous fertility: the same fawn will run
in a matter of weeks, wine pouring from heaven
          as sun and rain. In the riffles, brown trout
stuff themselves on sulphur and coffin flies.
          While we fish we watch the water's surface—
jaws parting, bodies porpoising, a thousand dimples
          and swirls that mimic the expanding galaxy.
In the sandy banks above the river, fox and mink
          dig for turtle eggs, yellow yolk dripping from chins,
their mates lapping the evidence to sate desire.
          My love and I sleep naked in the returned warmth,
hands draped over the round flesh of a long marriage,
          over the pleasure we take in each other's aging bodies.
Two nights ago a bear destroyed a friend's beehives,
          broke the boxes and left the drawers strewn
like half-read books. In the face of this wreckage
          he laughed, told me to think of the rapture
in a pink tongue swathed in honey, of the black-armed
          stickiness, the splendid apiary confusion: bees flying
everywhere, stinging the bear's immense head
          as he reared up and grinned, licking and grinding
the waxy comb between his teeth and gums.

Goat's Milk

The bells up and down the ridges
wander through the small window
in the kitchen wall. The girl who makes soap
and fudge from goat's milk to sell to tourists
who come for the fall foliage is trying to describe
for her mother, who is deaf, what it sounds like
when she slides her fingers along the slick udder
and milk spurts from the goat's nipple.
She makes no mention of the goat kid
they found mostly eaten in the rocks, how she
took the bell from around its neck and washed
the blood from the shiny metal with the hose
at the side of the house. Her father and brother
want to kill the coyote that did this, and part of her
wants that, too. She forms words with her hands,
gestures to her mother, and says with silent lips
the word *red*, because milk sounds alive to her,
and next the words *water* and *stone*, because the stream
running from the woods and into their pasture
resembles the clattering of hooves. The last word
she mouths, wrists turning over the expression
like needles knitting wool, is *risk*, the swish-
swish of milk circling the bottom of the pail,
a single goat neglected by her brother
who brought the herd from the far meadow,
the parting of grass as a paw pads
the soft turf, and the bleat from the back
of a goat's throat, moaning first out of hunger,
then out of fear.

After Twenty-Seven Years of Marriage

I imagine your soul is the texture of cantaloupe
as you bend over the tub to wash your hair.

100 million years is a long time to migrate, but
the warblers flying through the black gum trees

outside our window navigate the same space
as their ancestors. The cat, descended from Egypt,

sleeps in the crook of your legs
with the expectation that we will rub her

under the chin and down the bridge of her nose.
In the morning a storm sacrifices more than six

inches of rain, and now a cow bobs down the river,
rolling from side to side. You collected toy horses

as a child because your father was poor and drank away
the hay, the stall doors, the paddock fencing.

After correcting me about how your soul feels,
you feed me pink slices of watermelon.

I drown happily in the sweetness
of your company.

Native Species

At work he found himself looking at paintings of deer on the Internet. Some dead, some dying, others resting in tall grass or beneath green boughs, the gentle sound of water rolling over stone in the stream that bordered the picture and flowed out of the frame. Tracking a doe through briar and multiflora rose, he'd feel the ease of the deer's movements, the muscle that shaped kinship with the mountain. For him the trail was precarious, one boot in front of the other as he scaled steep talus or sunk to his waist in the sloggy alder swamps where many took refuge: cold soaking skin, changing his own scent. While laboring with a meat saw, he protested that he loved what he killed, offering elaborate prayers of thanksgiving for the animal that fed his family. When winter grew deep, he found the earthen bowls where they slept, heat of their bodies melting snow, and close by a shed antler, like a crown removed before sleep. Trimming a hang nail, he began to suspect something. Plate dark and thick, black as bituminous coal. He told his wife he'd banged his fingers in a door, but soon his toes divided as well—three to one side, two to the other, a slant with angular curves that made wearing shoes impractical. His wife insisted he see a doctor. Instead he went to the woods where his back bent and lengthened, neck drawn out, eyes brought to the side, dusky and knowing. Still she recognized him, clasped his face under the muzzle, scolded him for procrastinating, while pressing her forehead to his, stroking the coarse hair along his chest and belly. During rifle season, when the family heard a shot roll up the valley, they ran to the porch and called his name, waiting for the comfort of a tail's flash along treeline. His sons were careful to mark the shape of the ivory patch at the base of his throat and swore only to hunt squirrel and rabbit. His daughter, who loved to ride his shoulders, tied yellow yarn from his brow tines in a cat's cradle. Beneath moonlight, on late summer evenings, he ate the beets and clover she planted in the garden, stamped his hoof in dark soil, until a face appeared at the window to look down on velvet antlers, illuminated like branches in wet snow.

How Our Names Turn into Light

One man hammers stone

   in the middle of a quarry; another

cuts blocks from its side. In faraway cities

   monuments are constructed, and the abandoned

pit fills with water and fish. Grain by grain

   the mountains diminish. In one sacred story

Christ bends to write in the sand; today, in this place,

   clouds shadow goldenrod fringe: bees and flies

moan with the pleasures of pollen

   smeared on abdomens. With legs heavy

from treasure, it's difficult to remember

   that farther north polar bears starve

as sea-ice recedes. Where we've fractured

   the earth's scapula, grief shudders involuntarily

like an aspen leaf. Some would have us believe

   death is consensual. We should practice

gratefulness, as Basho did, who gave thanks

for teeth to chew his evening meal of dried salmon.

The wind erases most of what's written

in the sand. The rain washes the rest.

The Rain that Holds Light in the Trees

Two months ago ice stacked up along the river's banks, thin
panes flipped by the wind. Some of the glass still fractures,
glistening brighter in its brokenness.

My grandmother told me that deer store their souls in antlers
and in winter shed them, visible spirits returning to the bone
beneath the forehead. On the coldest days, shorn reeds whistle

a music composed from wind and hollow stubs, an improvised
panpipe showering the silence. Evolution folded our brains
back and forth like taffy, skulls expanding, neck muscles growing

to support the weight of thought. Our mothers' pelvises
accommodated the soul's stretching as well, loosening joints
and soft tissue, squeezing us into a world we've dissected

and categorized, yet still know so little about. In Australia
biologists observe black kites and brown falcons descending
along the periphery of wildfires: wing-beat and talon-grasp,

a burning branch transported to start new fires. Our desire
to know more, to carry more of what we know with us,
causes us to forget that time is a swirl of stars, a constellation

of galaxies, a dream we can't remember when we wake.
The hippocampus in squirrel allows them to remember
where they've cached acorns and hickory nuts, the same

spatial cognition that helps me write about the bend
where Loup Run turns west along a talus field, sun low,
piercing poles of moosewood and black birch. In a note

I found in an old journal, I place myself behind my father:
a boy trying to walk in footprints spaced too far apart.
My father, who was younger than I am today, was afraid

I might step on a copperhead as we picked blackberries
for the batter my mother poured into a greasy skillet, flour
butter-crisped like gold leaf. Along the banks where the last

of the river water is frozen, holding out against its own passing
and the water's rising, our tracks are washing away. Ravens
and crows fall to the field just beyond tree line, eating remnants

of last year's corn, then fly up to the tallest branches
where clouds gather, bringing with them the rain
that holds light in the trees.

The Turtle

For the Men and Women Murdered in the Emanuel African
Methodist Episcopal Church, Charleston, South Carolina

The snapping turtle that crosses the riffles
where I fish is older than I am and descends
from prehistory with lumbering steps.
The shell on its back carries the world
while parting the waters that rush
around us. Nine people were shot
in a church while praying. So many
sacred stories about how turtle
was formed, how out of darkness
stars began to shine, the sun gathering
planets to its breast. A child must be taught
hatred and how to love a gun. This turtle
will bury her eggs in the sand, then retreat
into the river to swim toward home.
In the deepest pools, I hear the voices
of the bereaved singing.

Coltrane Eclogue

You can play a shoestring if you're sincere.
—JOHN COLTRANE

Where the beak of a pileated opened a row
of holes down the length of a snag
wind blows across each notch,
angles of breathing, like Saint Coltrane
unfastening pearl and brass, exhalation
rushing through the neck of a saxophone,
bending into the sound that envelops
anyone with ears to hear. I've started to chant
a love supreme, although I'm alone,
more than four miles into the crease,
trying to pick up the rhythm, how each
lungful glides through hemlock needles,
kestrel slipping out onto the updraft,
with one wing-beat shifting the air
ever so slightly. And yet another woodpecker
drilling the side of a dying tree, a northern
flicker that stays just out of sight, laying down
a percussive line. I feel foolish for saying this,
but it's like being reborn, a syncopation
that can call down rain, make the bud of a shadbush
unfurl, unwrap the slow, honest tongues
of beaver, and stamp a moose's enormous
hind-quarter like a bass, all the others silenced,
fingers of that long-dead saint scaling gut-strings,
before a Blackburnian warbler joins in with its thin,
plaintive notes, and a goddamned bluebird,
which should seem trivial but is not, breast puffed,
raising its head toward a God that surrounds us,
who opens our stupid mouths and commands us
to play whatever instrument we've got.

Gnosis

In a blue river made of snowmelt
that forms this valley of aspen and alder,

I fish with my sons until summer's light fades
in the recesses of a canyon.

While hunting alone I entered a small cave
to take shelter from a passing squall

and found the bones of a bear cub
curled in a circle of trust.

Someday when the white fields disappear
and only rain falls from the heavens,

this river will vanish too.
The trout we catch have throats that shine

with a bright red mark, suggesting the role
blood plays in betrayal.

A woman who is long dead told me
that when a river passes away, it holds

the memory of itself in the silt left behind.
When our species is extinct,

what animal will carry the memory
of our lives?

Returning to Earth

At the bottom of an abandoned well
dug more than a century ago
the moon rises from the center
of the earth, a crust of ice
forming around its edges.

The stand of larch outside
our bedroom window
sways, golden needles
stirring the air
underneath its boughs.

I open the window to hear
the river sailing away, riding
the stone boat of the basin
carved by spring floods.

Beyond the faint light
of a candle, your voice asks
if we might touch and remember
how our children were made,
how the bodies of our parents
were returned to earth.

I want our children's hands
to hold the river, to watch it spill
through their fingers, back to a source
older than our names
for God.

Beneath a waxing moon
we've witnessed animals
dragging their dead into the light.
Tonight we imagine some
suckling their young
who are born blind
in these coldest months.

Soon the river will freeze,
and come morning we'll break
the ice in the well
so we may drink.

In dark's shelter I place the words
of a prayer upon your tongue.
You are gracious, saying
the prayer back
into my waiting mouth.

Thankful for Now

Walking the river back home at the end
of May, locust in bloom, an oriole flitting
through dusky crowns, and the early night sky
going peach, day's late glow the color of that fruit's
flesh, dribbling down over everything, christening
my sons, the two of them walking before me
after a day of fishing, one of them placing a hand
on the other's shoulder, pointing toward a planet
that's just appeared, or the swift movement
of that yellow and black bird disappearing
into the growing dark, and now the light, pink
as a crabapple's flower, and my legs tired
from wading the higher water, and the rocks
that keep turning over, nearly spilling me
into the river, but still thankful for now
when I have enough strength to stay
a few yards behind them, loving this time
of day that shows me the breadth
of their backs, their lean, strong legs
striding, how we all go on in this cold water,
heading home to the sound of the last few
trout splashing, as mayflies float
through the shadowed riffles.

from WINTERKILL

Homily

O I say these are not the parts and poems of the Body only,
but of the Soul,
O I say now these are the Soul!
—WALT WHITMAN

By the second week in September nuthatches capture the last
elderberries, excrement purpled and extravagant, sprayed
drunkenly across my truck's hood. I've been thinking about the God
I pray to with no lasting effect and note the effortless work
the stream does as it feeds these bushes. My father was baptized
in the Green River, led by the hand in white robes to be dunked
beneath the current. Sometimes when mother gathers sheets
from the clothesline in late summer, she finds the droppings
of a bluebird written like a sacred text. But what saint could decipher it?
In a field reclaimed by clover, I sprawl sideways and count
the small green hands of the leaves enfolding me. The gentle *sshh,*
sshh of the wind dismisses my garbled words as they break
the water's surface or cross over the low hum of bees. Eventually
we have to ascend to breathe, accepting the uncertainty of the air
above our heads. At dusk a skein of geese skitters in a half-formed V,
and a skulk of fox pups gnaw at each other's throats in a game
to prepare for death. Salvation is supposed to be sweet, like the sugar
of a wild grape, but where would we be without the fossil record to lead?
All of us are worth saving, despite the stink we've made since learning
to walk upright 400,000 years ago. As a boy, when a calf got scours,
my father would search the field for lamb's ear, collecting its velvet
leaves to better dress the open sores that ran the length of the flanks.
His mother told him mercy is all Jesus wants of anyone. I believe,
despite my unbelief. When the Belgian drapes its sorrel neck
across the paddock gate, I offer him two handfuls of clover
I painstakingly picked.

Thieves

We filch
happiness
from the seed
pods of touch-
me-nots,
the explosion
of their husks
as they curl
backward
to expose
the future,
the leap
forward
into dreaming
dust, into
waiting out
winter
with hopes
a speckled
horn
will blossom
and bees
will crawl
inside it
to blow
a coupled
music.

What My Neighbor Tells Me
Isn't Global Warming

Two hours west in Pittsburgh my friend's snow peas blossom, only
mid-April and his lettuce already good for three weeks. Whenever my
neighbor and I meet at our mailboxes, he tells me, *Global warming's a
bunch of bullshit*, the same way you or I might say, *How's the weather?* or,
Sure could use some rain. It's a strange salutation, but he's convinced the
president is a communist. I keep asking my wife if any of this is going
to change. I think she's tired of my questions. Yesterday our son wrote a
letter to give to his girlfriend after he breaks up. He says he's real sorry.
So am I. The tears they'll cry are no different than our cat's wailing to be
let out, despite the rain that's been falling since dawn. The three donkeys
that graze in the pasture share the field with exactly eleven horses. It's
instructive that the horses don't lord it over the donkeys that they're
horses. For two straight weeks in March it was thirty degrees warmer
than it should've been. Last night the moon shot up brighter than I've
ever seen it, a giant eyeball staring us down, or one of those lightbulbs
that's supposed to last for five years. The weatherman called it perigee
on the six o'clock news, so I walked to the pasture to see if it made any
difference to the donkeys. Each time a horse shuffled its hooves and
spread its legs to piss or fart, the shadow looked like a rocket lifting off.
Awe and wonder is what I feel after a quarter century of marriage. My
wife just shakes her head when I say her right ankle is like a wood lily's
stem, as silky and delicate as that flower's blossom. If she'd let me, I'd
slide my hand over her leg for hours without a trace of boredom. This
past week largemouth bass started spawning in the weeds close to shore,
patrolling back and forth with a singular focus. You can drag a popper
or buzzbait right in front of them and they'll ignore it. All this land we
live on was stripped for timber and coal a century ago. We still find
lumps, hard and black, beneath the skin. Now it's fracking for natural
gas. Can you imagine? We're actually breaking the plates on purpose. I
know what my grandmother would've said about that. Last time, before
the mining and timber companies pulled up stakes, they brought in

dozers that raked what little soil was left, planted thin grasses and pine trees. With the real forest gone, warm wind funnels through the gaps in the ridges, turns the giant turbine blades we've bolted to the tops of mountains.

Burn Barrel

A girl is throwing trash at the flames.
Anything that will burn. Plastic milk jugs,
cardboard boxes, the electric panels
of broken toys and the needled syringes
her mother uses to shoot insulin
into her thighs. The fire smolders, gray-
to-black-to-purple, mutating into a green
plume like the peacock feather she bought
when her class took a trip to the zoo.
She slips a caramel between her lips, stolen
from her grandmother's pink candy dish.
She watches snow fall and the wind blow
across the mouth of the barrel, whistling
smoke into a field of corn-stubble, shading
a trail to the edge of the woods where each day
it grows dark a little earlier. She hears
the snowplow on the county road, sees sparks
as the blade strikes asphalt. When her stick
stirs what's left of the flames, she feels
the sugar in her body rise against the barrel
that warms her. She feeds the fire
that melts the sky.

Sulphur Hatch

Tonight our son is on the river
that runs through the upper pasture.
The cattle low as he loops
a nearly invisible line
into the air.

Above the water sulphurs hatch
and trout begin to surface.
The sun descends between
a water gap that joins Bell's Run
to our river.

The sky this time of night
whitens to the color of a blackberry
blossom, and a kingfisher flies
out of a sycamore to dive
at the spine of a trout.

Yesterday we found a fish,
gray and stiff, at the clear bottom
of the stream. We tossed it
onto the bank, hoping a raccoon
might scavenge it.

In this half-light, our boy is walking
home across the early June hay.
Each step he takes
leaves a shadowed space
we'll see come morning.

By the Rivers of Babylon

The father of a boy my son plays basketball with
overdosed last week. Out of prison less than two days, he slid
the needle into that place where he wanted to feel something
like God and pushed the plunger of the syringe. The boy isn't any good
at sports, but when the coach subs him late in the game, score
already settled, we cheer wildly, as if he's performed a miracle,
when he makes a layup or snares a rebound. Heroin is sold
in narrow spaces between row houses in the first few blocks
that rise from the railroad tracks and train shops. This part of town
still looks like the 1950s, if the soft pastels of that decade
had crumbled to gravel and ash. The boy lives with his grandmother
in a curtained white house near the cathedral. His mother,
who lost custody when he was five, is back in jail for possession.
At the funeral, my son and his friends pat the boy on the shoulder,
mumble they're sorry after the mass, then usher him to the pizza shop
where they eat as many slices as their stomachs will hold.
In Pennsylvania, if you keep your eyes on the horizon,
the mountains look heavenly. The white lines that snake
through the gaps in winter become streams that hold
the most delicate fish. As the snowpack melts,
there's more water than we know what to do with,
all of it rushing toward the valley and the muddy river
whose banks keep washing away.

The Last Time My Mother Lay Down with My Father

How did he touch my mother's body
once he knew he was dying? Woods white
with Juneberry and the question of how
to kiss the perishing world, where to place
his arms and accept the gentle washing
of the flesh. With her breast in hand
did he forgive with some semblance
of joy the final bit of fragrance
in the passing hour, the overwhelming
sweetness of multiflora rose, and the press
of her skin against his?

The body's cartography is what we're given:
flesh sloughing into lines and folds, the contours
of its mapmaking. When at last he died,
summer's heat banking against the windows,
she'd been singing to him, her face near to his,
and because none of us wanted it to end,
we helped her climb into bed next to him
where she lifted his hand to her chest
and closed her eyes.

Poem Made of Sadness and Water

When the rescue divers found the boys
drowned in the river hole, twelve
feet deep and held under
by curved stone, which blocked
the sun so they could not tell
the direction their breath rose,
each had wrapped his arms
around his friend, the one
who dared the other to swim,
and the other, who, seeing
his friend row the air, then
vanish, leapt in, only to lose
his way in the current
that hid this strange place
from their parents
and where they spied
the yellow and red iridescence
trout store at their sides
and the muskrat's webbed
feet clawing the hole
in the bank's mud wall
and a willow log
with bits of black leaf
swirling around the dead
branches, which reminded them
of the tadpoles they caught
and kept in jelly jars.

Canticle for Native Brook Trout

Now we are all sitting here strangely
On top of the sunlight.
—JAMES WRIGHT

Fishing the narrow stream
of light, we follow a seam
between hemlock and sweating
rhododendron, tulip poplar
and white oak that grow
more than a hundred feet tall.
The small fish that have been here
for thousands of years
lay in on flat rock that lines
the streambed, or hide beneath
the shelves where water
pours over fallen trees.
They are nearly invisible,
backs colored like the stone
in the pool where they were born
and where they will die
after giving birth to their own.
The drift of our flies
tempts them, and through
the glass surface we see
their jaws part, predatory
surge ending with a struggle
to be freed from the end
of our lines. Their lives
depend upon the coldness
of water, upon our desire
to touch their bodies,
to marvel at the skin
along their spines: the tan
worm-shaped ovals,

the smallest red circles,
the splash of yellow
and orange that washes
around their bellies
as we release them
and they swim
from our grasp
back into a sliver
of sunlight.

from IN THE KINGDOM
OF THE DITCH

Taxonomy

We've been taken captive
by the world, named by it, taught

to eat from its table. The whetted blade
slides through the flesh, thin veil

that parts to reveal what we think
is the soul. We set fires and burn

the earth because berry canes
won't come back without dirt

as dark as the color of its fruit.
Before the oldest trees were felled

we traveled the watercourse.
Now in the open fields we track

coyote, hoping to save the sweet
lambs we tend. Sadly, as night

stumbles down, all we find
are clumps of wool caught

in teasel's fine comb.
More than two centuries ago

Linnaeus began to arrange all
the names we've given back

to the world. This is how we know
black walnut hulls, when crushed,

smell like lemon, or when we walk
through sweet fern grouse will burst

into flight, dragging the plant's sharp
scent into the air. Near the stream

a tulip poplar blows down, leaves
turning the yellow of mustard

and ragwort. Despite the order
we've cultivated, the charts

we've set to memory, we're likely
to discover our way is one

of unknowing. When we die
may we be a pleasing word

placed in the mouth
of the world.

What I Told My Sons after My Father Died

The emptiness of the catalpa flower's mouth opens
into nothing: stamen encased by cream.

My father called it a weed tree, despite his love
for the light it provided in June, the colors it caught

as dark came down over the garden we tended. The way
he told the story, after my great, great grandfather

escaped from a Confederate prison, he traveled north
by night along creekbeds. He rested beneath the draped

boughs of catalpa, drank branch water and ate pawpaws.
Supposedly in dark's false stillness he could tell the difference

between a hound and a groundhog, that in the water's hushed
movements he could pick out the stones breaking the surface

of the stream long before dawn woke those who hunted him.
In trying to explain the stillness, I don't wish to add

to my sons' sorrow. If I could play three notes
upon the fiddle, I'd do that instead. When my first boy

was born, in the nights after we brought him home,
I stood above his crib, head pressed over the rail

to assure myself he still breathed. I did the same
when I was a kid working at the animal hospital.

I'd open a cage, my ear flush with the chest
of a dachshund or Doberman and listen to the heart,

after the strain of surgery, as it settled back into a sound
like a kick wheel turning clay. My father taught me

the names for trees, which in turn I've taught my sons.
That's what it was like after he stopped breathing.

A bee disappears down the flower's mouth.
Although we can't see it, the bee's still there.

Apophatic

The mind is murky, mottled
from too many days of rain.
I miss the thrush's fluting
and realize it's not the earth
that's dying but my attachment
to it. The first writing
was on the body, then the skin
of trees—pokeberry crushed
and driven to ink. The fox's
track is delicate, and where the river
rose and spilled, it left an unreadable
script. What does it mean to take
something you've not been given?
In the dream evening primrose
blooms the first yellow of a broken
vessel, juniper like the olive
skin of those animals we christen.
The rattle of the catalpa pod opens
into sleep while in the orchard
I gaze up at red planets adrift in space.
Does the doe dream of this place?
And the dog whose hind legs twitch
in sleep as he gives chase?
The field beyond the orchard
lies fallow, and orange and black
beetles devour milkweed,
laying eggs that will hatch
on the undersides of leaves
long after their deaths.

Fishing for Large Mouth in a
Strip-Mining Reclamation Pond
near Lloydsville, Pennsylvania

The gills rake down the sides of his head, and the mouth
opens like the tunnels we used before the coal companies

hauled in dozers and trucks to scrape away the mountain
our grandparents had known. There was honor in riding

rail cars underground, something mythic as fathers said
goodbye to their children and traveled away from the sun.

Our teachers told us the story of Sisyphus, and we understood
how a stone might roll back upon the one who pushed it.

Most of the tunnels are gone, filled in or forgotten, holes
in our memory where the black line of money vanished

like the wind that sweeps over the backside of the Alleghenies.
As penance the state made us dig out this pond in the shape

of a kidney, water the color of liver, banks covered in cattails
and loosestrife. On the mounds of dirt that were left, goldenrod

grows in thin circles, like yellow mustard on bologna, the white
bread of cloudy skies balanced on the horizon where red oak

and hemlock should be. Black birch is the only tree
that comes up, rises toward the sun's lure, like a bass striking

the plastic popper my son dragged across the pond's surface, bait
imitating a frog's ragged dance, enticing this fish he hooked

and grips by the lower lip, both of them smiling, or grimacing,
or simply trying to hold still for the camera.

The Poet Stumbles upon a Buddha in Game Lands 158 above Tipton, Pennsylvania

A young boar (*Ursus americanus*) rests his rump

      on the pliable beam of a devil's walking stick, bending

the tree halfway to the ground so he might claw black

      and purple pebbles from its crown into a mouth as large

as a bushel-basket, tongue turned dark as the sweet scat

      he leaves in the middle of the path, a host of berries

littering his belly, and his great head reared back

      in a grin, no concern for abundance or waste or

for what comes after this early September light,

      which filters down through yellow poplar leaves, wind

making a sound like temple bells caught seventy feet up

      in the canopy.

Crow Counsels Me in the Ways of Love

Crow comes to the garden, lands
near the largest cantaloupe, proceeds
to walk back and forth, head shaking
from side to side. Crow talks incessantly
while I pick weeds from around tomato vines,
the leafy tops of turnips, the oblong peppers
that touch the earth like fallen breasts, or
a drooping cock. Crow says rain will fall
this afternoon, suggests I wait to weed:
wet earth makes such work go with ease.
In his torn voice Crow is forever
giving advice. Last week, after fighting
with you, Crow counseled me, said to pick
a cup of raspberries, to lay them in a circle
atop your bowl of cereal.

Nurse Log

Bend back the bark of the world,
which is its skin, which is the way
we learn how veins carry blood
away from the heart, then back
into its echoing chambers. I'm tired
of hearing about the kind of men
who would kill me, the news of bombs
going off in endless loops on late-night TV.
In the forest above our house a fisher
stalks porcupines, and every so often
I find their torn bodies, once even
a corpse in the crotch of a white oak.
Its animal face lay open, empty and red
where the fisher's teeth had bitten down
to avoid the quills and to keep
the belly meat untouched. In nature
there is waste that good grows out of,
an abundance we are called to use.
In spring when we coax the bees
toward a new hive, Alverdia fetches
her wooden spoon and metal washbasin,
stands beneath the shad and pawpaw trees
whose blossoms the bees cover,
whose limbs sprout ten thousand wings,
and there she drums the basin
and hums a song she's made
for herself and for this swarm
that will follow her anywhere.
This isn't the news of the world
most of us live in. Two streams
meet in the floodplain where wet fires
of rot lap against fallen hemlocks.

Five seedlings have sprung up
along one of the logs, nursing decay
like piglets down a sow's length, or like
an infant in a desert village suckling
a mother's breast, oblivious to the murmur
of planes crossing overhead.

The Sound of Sunlight

On the far side
of the canyon
light
is burning
through two
draws
like water
rushing
into an empty
riverbed.

A canyon wren
opens
her mouth
and a coyote
stops
midtrail
before vanishing
among juniper.

As we descend
the eastern wall
we look
down
onto
ponderosa
pine
and witness
the shadow
of a merlin
chase
the merlin
itself.

Behind us
in the meadow
where we lay
last night
the squall
of an elk
picks up
the sound
of sunlight
and joins it
in a flood
of bugling.

A Prayer for My Sons, after a Line of Reported
Conversation by the Poet William Blake to a Child
Seated Next to Him at a Dinner Party

If I could send the sun
sprawling from my mouth,
if each night the moon might drop

from my eyes onto your head,
if I could reach up and take a star
whose light has traveled toward you

for thousands of years and place it
under the bed where you sleep,
I would do all these things. But

being a man who has seen
no angels and who at times doubts
what he's been told in church,

I'll simply ask what the Poet asked—
that God would make this world
as beautiful to you as it has been to me.

from THE LEAST OF THESE

Doctrine

I love the church
of the osprey, simple
adoration, no haggling
over the body, the blood,
whether water sprinkled
from talons or immersed
in the river saves us,
whether ascension
is metaphor or literal,
because, of course,
it's both: wings crooked,
all the angels crying out,
rising up from nests
made of sticks
and sunlight.

April Poem

In the book that rests in my lap, Issa notes
passing geese, Basho the scroll of clouds.

The calligrapher's brush paints the dark
edge of a spring storm while Amish turn

the earth—thud of draft horses' hooves,
sound of plow striking stone. Two women,

heads covered, travel by buggy to town
where they will buy fabric for the dresses

they sew. Somewhere behind the hill's shadow
Tu Fu laughs, draws a line in the dirt, composes

a poem about cherry blossoms pitched in the wind,
their petals clinging to fresh horse dung.

Questions for the Artist

You keep taking things
out of your pictures, erasing
the superfluous—a dog
at rest, a cake half-eaten,
even the snow that fell
last night and now recedes
into the withering grass,
which you paint
the yellow
of a recovering bruise.
Why bother to keep
the thin line
of a barbed wire fence,
the heavy chain
of a half-worked log?
What's so essential
about faded wallpaper,
a knife and plate,
a plain saucer
holding a cup?

After Andrew Wyeth's "Groundhog Day" (1959)

The Face of Jesus

Weasel wears the happy face of Jesus, yolk smeared
at the smiling corners of his mouth. Like Mary Magdalene
these hens give what is most precious, his feet perfumed

by egg whites. Opossum wears the sad face of Jesus, eyes
sleepy with death. Already his brother lies on his back, the red
part of his life making the sign of the cross against a hash mark.

Fox wears the sly face of Jesus, speaks in parables about cold nights
and days covered in the silence of white fields. Coyote wears
the laughing face of Jesus. The men in the hill country hunt him

because he breaks the body of the yearling doe, gives thanks and sips
from the cup of her blood. Bear wears the sleepy face of Jesus,
belly bloated with huckleberries and nuts, with the fish

he catches in the net of his claws. Squirrel wears the wary face
of Jesus, knows the wind will betray him like Judas, all the acorns
rotting, Owl plotting against his life.

Ananias Lays Hands on Saul

The light, which left a scrim of salt
upon my skin, was speaking, and the voice

addressed me with the noise wind makes
in weeds or the drumming of bulrushes.

When it ceased, I could not see,
and my companions took me by the arms

into the city where in a room made of mudbricks
the voice returned, this time as ice and snow

strafed to the sides of leaves. For three days
I did not eat or drink, quiet as I considered

the pair of ravens that were my hands. Then,
another pair of hands, like the useless, forgotten

wings of a hen, touching the sides of my face,
and the scales, which were not like the snake's

sloughed skin but like the sheerest yellow petal
of the flower that grows near water's edge,

falling from my eyes and becoming dust.

Confession

Forgive me
they were delicious
—WILLIAM CARLOS WILLIAMS

Like Williams and his plums, meat
turning to sugar under skin, I confess

my sin: I've eaten the apples
that ferment in tall grass, abandoned

when the life fell out of the place.
With the first cold days, at night

they freeze, then thaw a bit by noon,
last warmth of October

drawing these few incorrigible bees
who still bother to venture across

this rotting round globe.

Puberty

Among the last of the raspberries
we find scat seeded about, canes
pushed over without care, tufts of hair
sticking to the black juice of berries.
Arms carry the proof of hours
reaching between thorns, lower leaves
pushed aside to find the darkest,
ripest part of our delight. My son,
who has begun to change, stands
thirty yards away, picks disinterestedly,
asking how soon before we can leave.
Hair sprouts everywhere on his body:
forearms, legs, balls. When you're older
there's more in the nose and ears, eyebrows
gone mad. I'd like to say this siren song
that calls him away will disappear in time,
music fading into the hollow bend of a tree,
but no one knows where the notes will lead him.
Instead I bow my head, a penitent working
through prayers to the sweet forgiveness
of this precious wood that feeds us, to these
brief moments we have before this boy refuses
to spend even a few hours in our company.
It's his shout that interrupts my failed attempt
at something holy, that brings me around
to his jabbing finger, harried eyes pointing
to a young bear scrambling across the path
and into the brush. In the silence that follows
the crash, I'm afraid I've lost something
I won't be able to retrieve, though I know
my son still stands among these brambles.

Accident

They tell the son, who tells his friends
at school, that the father's death was
an accident, that the rifle went off
while he was cleaning it. I'm not sure
why he couldn't wait. We understand
the ones who decide to leave us in February,
even as late as March. Snows swell.
Sun disappears. Hunting season ends.
With two deer in the freezer any family
can survive. I know sometimes
it feels like you've come to the end
of something. Sometimes you just want
to sit down beneath a hemlock and never go
back. But this late in the year, when plum
trees have opened their blossoms?
Yesterday it was so warm we slept
with the windows open. Smell of forsythia
right there in the room. I swear
you could hear the last few open,
silk petals come undone, a soft sound
like a pad sliding through a gun's barrel,
white cloth soaked in bore cleaner,
removing the lead, the copper, the carbon
that fouls everything. My son knows
you don't die cleaning your rifle:
the chamber's always open.
I told him to nod his head anyway
when his friend tells the story,
to say *yes* as many times as it takes,
to never forget the smell of smoke
and concrete, the little bit of light
one bulb gives off in a basement
with no windows.

Letter to Galway Kinnell at the End of September

I confuse the name for goldenrod with the name for this month,
but what else would we call this time of year—afternoon light
like saffron, blue lake reflecting blue sky? Where we entered,
asters and goldenrod flooded the length of the meadow, field

literally abuzz, swaying with the movement of bees, air
warm enough to draw sweat and the smell of those flowers
and our bodies drifting around us. The part of the sun that rested
the kettle of heat upon the goldenrod's tiny, yellow blossoms

lifted the clearing clean out of the ground, somehow suspending us—
if not in air, then in time—and that's what we want after all.
Not starting over, not being reborn, but borne up like these bees,
or the birds who migrate toward a place of neverending, all of us

unmoored, still part of the earth, but absolved of our obligations to it:
the necessity of growing old, the bald fact that a month from now
all this beauty will crumble—asters black, goldenrod brown,
no more than flower-dust when we rake our hands across their heads.

Tree of Heaven

In my dream the pond opens at the center
of the field, and the field itself overflows
with the white heads of Queen Anne's lace.
When night comes on the water dims,
and it's impossible to tell where the clouds
reflected in the pond conclude and where
the flowers of the field commence. I'm certain
if I walk near the edge of the pond
I'll be pulled in, dragged downward
into its fullness. It's clear there's a choice
to be made, but I'm not ready to make it.

Years ago when I lived in Illinois I was
called to serve on a jury at a coroner's inquest.
We were told it was our job to determine
whether the deaths were accidents or suicides.
For some, money was at stake; for others,
salvation. If the death was an accident,
the insurance company could pay
what the policy said the life was worth;
if it was planned, the priest said the soul
could not enter heaven. That day in the room
with seven others—farmers and housewives
and teachers—I saw photographs and slides,
learned the way in death the body slumps
in a tub, the places in the ceiling where
you'll find bits of skull embedded
if the angle of the gun is right.
We were advised of the make and model
of cars, informed if a hose was wrapped
around the muffler and strung
through the rear window. Who is to say

whether a mother put her head in the oven
out of sadness, or because she was cleaning it
and didn't realize the gas was on
or the pilot light out? Because I was a teacher
I knew some of the families whose hopes
hung like a noose around our decisions.
Days later when I returned to my classroom,
I didn't say where I'd been. I picked up
the lesson right where we left off—
Hemingway's story about fishing
in northern Michigan after the war.

We continue to dream some dreams for years.
From the second grade until high school graduation
I dreamt of Judy Garland running through fields
of poppies. When you live with a dream for that long,
certain things disappear, others are added. For instance,
the pond, even when the night is its blackest, doesn't tug
at me anymore. And now there's a field of poppies
where once it was Queen Anne's lace. As I walk
through the field sometimes I find a ruby slipper
or a tuft of hair. As much as I wish for Judy Garland,
she never appears.

Now when I dream, at the top of a distant hill
there's a grove of ailanthus, better known
as tree of heaven. Brought over from China
more than a century ago, it spreads quickly,
nothing more than a trash tree whose roots
break apart drains, invading wells and springs.
Every year I cut and drag and burn it. Every year
there's more. I must admit, even though their flowers

are wretched, the fruit is a beautiful reddish-green,
and the tree's arms sprawl like the ones
we don't know the names for in *National Geographic*.

Sometimes I'm sorry for what I do, and for what others do
as well. Sometimes I wish it was all an accident, or a dream.
But when I think about the way these trees keep coming back,
the way they take over everything—topple old barns, consume
rusted tractors, wrecked plows and baling machines—I can't help
believing, like a tornado in Kansas, the wideness of heaven
might hold us all.

from SOME HEAVEN

The Possibility of Rain

Late August, yet farmers are already in their fields.
Rain hasn't fallen since June, leaving us nothing
but the harvest: beans hard as bbs, cornstalks brittle
as bone in the wake of summer's relentless heat.
As I drive home through the dark, I see the fires
have begun—sparks from combines to blame.
I pull out of the way of the sirens that wail on
into the growing black, smoke billowing
from the field to the back of Yoder's barn.
These men who come from town know
such conflagrations will build toward heaven
despite their best efforts. But who among us
can stop believing in the possibility of rain?
Dust rises from gravel roads with our nervous
movement, our need to work, and then catches
in the backs of our throats. For the past three
weeks, each night we wake and walk barefoot
through tall grass, heavy dew brushing the inside
of our thighs. An entire town up an hour before
daybreak, hiking toward the western skyline
where we believe thunderheads build, great
bellies of rain that promise something better
but only leave us miles from home.

Somewhere Else

Your house sank down toward the swamps
south of Bulldog Crossing, trains hollering
each night on the other side of the water, light
trailing across duckweed, lily pads, the bass
who swam in and out of the rotten trunk of an elm.
By fourth grade you were drinking Pabst
on the front porch. Father gone most of the month
with Conrail, his days and nights shuttled back
and forth between Chicago and St. Louis,
and your mother too drunk to care much about
her oldest boy taking to her ways: smoking
Lucky Strikes and cursing Jesus, hitting
the other kids who sat fixed before the blue glow
of the TV. I can't even say you were different
after the Accra Pac Plant blew—neighbor burnt
so bad they bandaged him head to foot, you calling
him Mummy, making fun of his mumble, the fact
he had to have seven surgeries to get his lips back.
No, long before that you told me this was all there was:
we could play football in high school; we could get high
and take our place in line at the factory. We did play.
You were noseguard. I was tackle. You were drunk
half the practices, but come game time you were more
than sober, hyped on speed, somehow determined to show
everybody that if life was fair, you'd kick it through
the uprights, live over on Greenleaf Boulevard
like the pricks who owned the factories, drove
their Cadillacs like it was something religious.
You said if you had what they had, you'd be fishing
most days from a pontoon, red and green lights
reflected in the St. Joe, instead of sitting here
in the dark. Cane pole propped in a cement block,

bass not biting, a 48-ounce open and half drained,
broken glass sticking up in the gravel that slopes away
from the railroad where last January you stepped
in front of the train that runs less frequently
these days, goddamn trucks carrying more
and more of the weight to somewhere else.

Prayer Requests at a Mennonite Church

Pray for the Smucker family. Their son Nathaniel's coat and shirt were caught in the gears while grinding grain. Nothing would give, so now he is gone. We made his clothes too well. Perhaps this is our sin.

Pray for the Birky family. Their son Jacob fell to his death in the granary. He was covered in corn before they could stop the pouring—chest crushed by the weight, seed spilling from his mouth. We hope something will grow from this, besides our grief.

Pray for the Hartzler family. Their youngest has left the church and no longer believes that Christ died for her sins. She buys clothes at the mall. Tongue pierced, nose as well. Her shirt shows her belly where a ring of gold sprouts. We pray she will remember that her Lord's side was pierced, that his crown held no gold, only the dried blood of his brow.

Pray for the Miller family. Last week their daughter, who lives in Kalona, lost her baby at birth. Child only half-formed: head turned the wrong way; heart laid on the outside of her chest; one leg little more than an afterthought. Lord, help them know that life may come again, that we are all made whole in heaven.

Pray for the Stutzman family. Their son fights in the war. We call him back to the Prince of Peace, to our Savior who knelt to gather the slave's ear, brushed the dirt away, lifted it to the side of his flushed face. May we leave no scars. May we ask no blessing for the killing done in His name.

Sleep

On the ridge above Skelp Road
bear binge on blackberries and apples,
even grapes, knocking down
the Petersens' arbor to satisfy the sweet
hunger that consumes them. Just like us
they know the day must come when
the heart slows, when to take one
more step would mean the end of things
as they should be. Sleep is a drug;
dreams its succor. How better to drift
toward another world but with leaves
falling, their warmth draping us,
our stomachs full and fat with summer?

Jacklighting

In this part of Pennsylvania, roads run along
streambeds, or beside the narrow tributaries
the highest ridges conceal when they turn
their faces to the north or south—creases

marked the length of their long necks, ravines
as beautiful as the shadowed space at the base
of a woman's throat. In these little-traveled
places, the men who have been without work

for weeks and weeks take their trucks out
into the dark to find deer, to capture them
in the gaze of their highbeams, so they might
kill, come back to their homes with more

than the defeated faces they wear as they pay
for milk and bread with food stamps, their few
real dollars laid down for a pack of Camels
they'll smoke as they gut the animal in the barn,

taking what they can, dumping the rest along
the river where winter snows bury the arcs
of the deer's slender white ribs.

After Andrew Wyeth's "Jacklight" (1980)

Some Heaven

The rabbit's head is caught
between the slats of the fence,
and in its struggle it has turned
so the hind legs nearly touch
the nose—neck broken, lungs failing.
My boys ask me to do something
but see no mercy in my plan.
At five and eight, they are so far
away from their own deaths
that they cannot imagine the blessing
a shovel might hold, the lesson
suffering offers those who have
not suffered.

At bedtime, my youngest prays
the rabbit is in a heaven
where there are no fences, where
there is more than enough to eat.
He begins to cry and we rock
until sleep's embrace takes him
from me. I know his prayer is right.
What more should heaven be?
A place wild with carrot and dill,
sunflower and phlox, fields
that stretch on for miles, every coyote
full, every hawk passing over, a warm
October day that need never end.

from RIPE

For an Uncle, Twenty-Four Years after His Passing

I.

I thought I saw you this morning,
a glimpse in Larson's field
where they began the harvest
at first light—sun rising from acres of dry corn,
combine sending smoke toward sky
and the wide open, blue, seemingly everlasting,
cut by the dust of tractors and wagons
vanishing toward the farthest farm.

II.

But their cutting, spewing—
organized as the ants on the back porch—
kept me from seeing if you recognized me.
Moving down rows, precise, deft,
the machines devoured June suns,
spitting golden worlds into the truck bed
that rolled on beside.
You were gone, hidden by their work,
and I let the car roll forward,
on toward school, the coming day,
the stories of the past.

III.

I tell my class of you.
Your drink: the thirst of a giant
taking beer, wine, whiskey,
even aftershave,
to forget, to survive.
But unlike your brothers, your sisters,
it was always the harvest that would
not be forgotten.
Your sister's twin dead at two,
lost in a stumble . . . the laundry water boiled,
placed on the kitchen floor.
And for you, as for me,
things are forever fumbling forward.

IV.

You often talked of country matters
with fond admiration: the field, dark
under an October moon, filled
with the remains of harvest past,
turned under for November rains
and winter snows, for life's sweet
decay, for lastness.
But the country was never yours.
Louisville, the service, and forever
back to Louisville. And when you left,
your autopsy told us that you'd been dying
for years—liver and kidneys and heart,
large with the scars of drinking,
harvesting your life slowly.

V.

I, too, talk of country matters,
my wife riding with me in the dark,
the day left behind at the university.
I have a fond admiration for what will never be mine:
the soil—pushed over, turned under—waiting
for spring rain, summer growth,
for doves and crows who will sit on stalks,
rigid with life, with eventual death,
and I am reminded that we never met.

VI.

Still,
morning always has a way of coming again,
and in the early dawn,
as I drive by the empty field,
I see that, yes, it is you,
sprawled on broken corn stalks,
the first light snow of winter
falling slowly on you
like bits of heaven.

Fear of Flying

I got over mine
one March
coming into Atlanta
in the dark,
city lights strewn
like the torn tails
of fireflies.

Wings shuddered and bounced,
scudded against air,
plane tilting, then dropping:
streets snaking
through neighborhoods,
cars flashing,
and the earth,
which seemed so solid,
beneath it all.

In our descent,
drafts lifted us,
pushed us from
the light of living
rooms and streetlamps,
and I began to realize
that my fear was not
of flight itself
but departure.

What made the difference,
finally, was a blessing:
the knowledge
that all must return—
whether one day, bent by age
and digging in the garden,
or, on another, too young,
yet falling
from the sky,
metal turned
toward darkness,
stars spinning,
while far below,
illuminated
by their own flowering,
white hands of dogwood,
faint traces of blood
and memory rising.

Building Walls

At the edge of our woods,
when the trees begin to green
and you say
        it is time to go for stone,
        the rocks begin to surface.

They grow large in surrounding fields,
backs of the baptized
cleaned by storms,
        and their weight, pushing toward blue,
        settles darkly.

In late afternoon we sweat
with the effort of moving stone from earth
while spring sun,
        still pushed to the far horizon,
        begins to take our working light.

Rusted wheelbarrow carries what will be today's last load,
and together, where our field ends and the world begins,
we touch,
        shoulder to shoulder,
        fitting stone upon stone.

The Blind Man

is led by his dog onto the bus
across the street from the baggage claim
at O'Hare. The only open seat left
is halfway back on the right side,
but the dog knows what to do
and does it well and soon we
are in motion. Across the aisle
a young Indian boy grins
at his father, points at the dog
with quick, furtive movements,
giggles at the harness, at the way
the canine's ears drape his head.
The father leans over and explains
to the blind man that his son
has just arrived in America and has never
seen anyone led by a dog. Another man
two seats back reaches forward to get
the boy's attention and proudly tells him
that the dog knows forty-five different
words and signs, that he understands
better than most of us could.

Later in the trip, the same man notices
that I'm not asleep and begins to tell
me a story about how he once trained
seeing-eye dogs. He describes the kennels
housed in the garage behind his house,
the concrete floors that would sweat
in summer, the drains that clogged
with shit and hair and scraps of unwanted
food and how he had to dig it all out

at least once a week so the water would
again move freely when he sprayed
down the runs with the garden hose.

For a moment he cannot speak,
and when he begins again, his hands
tremble as he tells me about his wife—
her hair, how before it fell from her head
during chemo it was the beautiful brown
and gold of the blind man's shepherd;
how she would find injured birds, squirrels,
raccoons, even skunks, and nurse them;
how he buried her nearly five years ago
yet nothing seems to stay in the ground.

At a convenience store in Gary, we both
get sandwiches sealed in plastic wrap.
He drinks coffee, he says, because
he doesn't like to sleep when the bus
is moving: it reminds him too much
of long trips with her. Not far
from South Bend, just as I begin
to nod off into a dream of my own wife
and our sons, he bends toward my ear
and whispers—as if what he tells me must
be kept quiet—that the reason he lost
his business, or, he corrects himself, the reason
he had to give it up, was because of dogs
like the one that now rests its head in the hands
of the small, dark boy—he just couldn't stand
each year having to give away
all that he had seen.

Acknowledgments

My thanks to the editors of the following journals or publications in which these poems first appeared, sometimes in different form.

———————

32 Poems: "For a Stray Dog near the Paper Mill in Tyrone, Pennsylvania"

5 AM: "A Prayer for My Sons, after a Line of Reported Conversation by the Poet William Blake to a Child Seated Next to Him at a Dinner Party"

Alaska Quarterly Review: "Goat's Milk"

American Literary Review: "Pit Ponies"

American Poetry Review: "The Poet Stumbles upon a Buddha in Game Lands 158 above Tipton, Pennsylvania"

Appalachia: "Sleep"

Arts & Letters: "Burn Barrel," "By the Rivers of Babylon," "The Dam on Loup Run," and "The Bear inside the Bear"

Atlanta Review: "The Sound of Sunlight"

Barrow Street: "Almanac of Faithful Negotiations"

basalt: "dream elevator"

The Basilica Review: "Letter to Galway Kinnell at the End of September"

Chariton Review: "After Twenty-Seven Years of Marriage"

Chautauqua: "Of This Failing" and "The Last Time My Mother Lay Down with My Father"

Christianity & Literature: "The Face of Jesus"

Cold Mountain Review: "How Our Names Turn into Light"

Cutthroat: "This Shared Life" and "Silt Psalm"

EcoTheo Review: "The Doctor Asks My Friend to Follow the Light at the End of Her Pen" and "Vernal Pond"

Ecotone: "Nurse Log"

Flyway: "Some Heaven"

The Fourth River: "Questions for the Artist"

The Gettysburg Review: "Ananias Lays Hands on Saul," "Buck Day," and "Decadence"

Gray's Sporting Journal: "After the Elk Hunt" and "Sulphur Hatch"

Green Mountains Review: "Puberty"

The Greensboro Review: "April Prayer"

Hampden-Sydney Poetry Review: "Apophatic" and "Coffin Honey"

Hayden's Ferry Review: "What My Neighbor Tells Me Isn't Global Warming"

Image: "Homily" and "Prayer Requests at a Mennonite Church"

Indiana Review: "Accident"

The Iowa Review: "April Poem"

The Journal: "Fishing for Large Mouth in a Strip-Mining Reclamation Pond near Lloydsville, Pennsylvania"

The Louisville Review: "Fishing with My Seventeen-Year-Old Self" and "The Turtle"

MidAmerica: "Tree of Heaven"

The Midwest Quarterly: "The Possibility of Rain"

The Missouri Review: "Mother," "Taxidermy: *Cathartes aura*" and "Wayfaring"

Natural Bridge: "Fear of Flying" and "Taxonomy"

The Nebraska Review: "The Blind Man"

North American Review: "Before My Mother's Funeral," "The Rain that Holds Light in the Trees," and "What I Know about the Last Lynching in Jeff Davis County"

Northern Appalachia Review: "Midsentence"

Notre Dame Review: "Goat Dream"

Orion: "Doctrine," "Sitting Shiva," and "Thieves"

Poet Lore: "Bear-Eater" and "Poem Made of Sadness and Water"

Poetry East: "Free Write"

Poetry Northwest: "Coltrane Eclogue" and "Until Darkness Comes"

Prairie Schooner: "Bare Limbs" and "Ditch Memory"

Qarrtsiluni: "Confession"

Radix Magazine: "For an Uncle, Twenty-Four Years after His Passing"

Raleigh Review: "The Taxidermist's Daughter Retrieves a Head"

Rhubarb (Canada): "Crow Counsels Me in the Ways of Love"

River Styx: "What I Told My Sons after My Father Died"

Ruminate: "Returning to Earth"

Southern Humanities Review: "Eclogue for an Extractive Economy"

Tar River Poetry: "Reservoir/Crows/Climate Change"

Terrain.org: "Canticle for Native Brook Trout" and "In the Garden"

Water~Stone Review: "Deposition: What Was Lost"
Western Humanities Review: "Field Sermon" and "Ursus in the Underworld"
Willow Springs: "Possum"
Yankee: "Building Walls"

"Apostate" was published in *The Ecopoetry Anthology: Volume II*, ed. Ann Fisher Wirth and Laura-Gray Street (San Antonio, TX: Trinity University Press, 2025).

"Confession" was published in *Visiting Dr. Williams: Poems Inspired by the Life and Work of William Carlos Williams*, ed. Thom Tammaro and Sheila Coghill (Iowa City, IA: University of Iowa Press, 2011).

"Fishing with Nightcrawlers" was published in *More in Time: A Tribute to Ted Kooser*, ed. Marco Abel, Jessica Poli, and Timothy Schaffert (Lincoln, NE: University of Nebraska Press, 2021).

"Gnosis" was published in *River Poems: Everyman's Pocket Classics*, ed. Henry Hughes (New York: Knopf, 2022).

"In the Garden" was published in *Dear America: Letters of Hope, Habitat, Defiance, and Democracy*, ed. Derek Sheffield, Simmons Buntin, and Elizabeth Dodd (San Antonio, TX: Trinity University Press, 2020).

"Thankful for Now" was published in *How to Love the World: Poems of Gratitude and Hope*, ed. James Crews (North Adams, MA: Storey Publishing, 2021).

"Tributary" was published in *The Art of Revising Poetry: 21 US Poets on their Drafts, Craft, and Process*, ed. Kim Stafford and Charles Finn (London, UK: Bloomsbury, 2023).

"Sleep" and "Thankful for Now" were featured in *American Life in Poetry* by Ted Kooser.

"Possum" was featured on *The Slowdown* by Major Jackson.

"Canticle for Native Brook Trout," "Eclogue for an Extractive Economy," and "The Sound of Sunlight" were featured by *Poetry Daily*.

"April Prayer," "For a Stray Dog near the Paper Mill in Tyrone, Pennsylvania," and "Thieves" were featured by *Verse Daily*.

"Prayer Requests at a Mennonite Church" and "The Sound of Sunlight" were featured by Garrison Keillor on *The Writer's Almanac*.

"Jacklighting" was featured on a poster as part of the Pennsylvania Center for the Book's Public Poetry Project.

"The Last Time My Mother Lay Down with My Father" was awarded the Editors Prize from *Chautauqua*.

"Tree of Heaven" was awarded the Gwendolyn Brooks Poetry Prize from the Society for the Study of Midwestern Literature.

"What I Know about the Last Lynching in Jeff Davis County" was selected as runner-up by Maggie Smith for the James Hearst Poetry Prize from *North American Review*.

———————————

All translations of the quoted lines from Po Chü-i, Tu Fu, and Yang Wan-Li are by David Hinton.

———————————

Thanks to the following people for their continued encouragement as I make my poems: Rick Bass, Jan Beatty, Lori Bechtel-Wherry, Tanya and Wendell Berry, Brian Black, Craig Blietz, Dave Bonta, Taylor Brorby, Lauren Camp, James Crews, Jim Daniels, Geffrey Davis, Joyce Davis, Nathan Davis, Noah Davis, Shelly Davis, Alison Hawthorne Deming, Chris Dombrowski, David James Duncan, Don Flenar, Don and Punky Fox, Michael Garrigan, Ross Gay, Dan Gerber, Andy Gottlieb, Leah Naomi Green, Jeff Gundy, Katie Hays, Jane Hirshfield, Henry Hughes, Jonathan Johnson, David Joy, Virginia Kasamis, Julia Spicher Kasdorf, Helen Kiklevich, Ted Kooser, Chris La Tray, Daniel Lassell, Carolyn Mahan, Adrian Matejka, Shara McCallum, Anne Haven McDonnell, Doug Miller, Dinty Moore, Erin Murphy, Aimee Nezhukumatathil, Lee Peterson, Ron Rash, Mary Rose O'Reilley, Sean Prentiss, Jack Ridl, Pattiann Rogers, Scott Russell Sanders, Derek Sheffield, Steve Sherrill, Dave Shumate, Jordan Temchack, Melanie Viets, Patricia Jabbeh Wesley, and Ken Womack.

Many of these poems were finished with the assistance of generous grants from the Pennsylvania State University.

TODD DAVIS is the author of seven full-length collections of poetry—*Coffin Honey*; *Native Species*; *Winterkill*; *In the Kingdom of the Ditch*; *The Least of These*; *Some Heaven*; and *Ripe*—as well as of a limited-edition chapbook, *Household of Water, Moon, and Snow*. He edited the nonfiction collection, *Fast Break to Line Break: Poets on the Art of Basketball*, and co-edited the anthologies *A Literary Field Guide to Northern Appalachia* and *Making Poems: Forty Poems with Commentary by the Poets*. His writing has won the Midwest Book Award, the Gwendolyn Brooks Poetry Prize, the Chautauqua Editors Prize, the Bloomsburg University Book Prize, and the Foreword INDIES Book of the Year Silver and Bronze Awards. His poems appear in such noted journals and magazines as *American Poetry Review*, *Alaska Quarterly Review*, *Iowa Review*, *North American Review*, *Missouri Review*, *Gettysburg Review*, *Orion*, *Prairie Schooner*, *Southern Humanities Review*, *Western Humanities Review*, *Verse Daily*, and *Poetry Daily*. He is an emeritus fellow of the Black Earth Institute and teaches environmental studies, creative writing, and American literature at Pennsylvania State University's Altoona College.